Cambridge Elements

Elements in Construction Grammar
edited by
Thomas Hoffmann
Catholic University of Eichstätt-Ingolstadt
Alexander Bergs
Osnabrück University

THE MEANING OF CONSTRUCTIONS

Benoît Leclercq
University of Lille

Cameron Morin
University of Paris-Cité

CAMBRIDGE
UNIVERSITY PRESS

Shaftesbury Road, Cambridge CB2 8EA, United Kingdom

One Liberty Plaza, 20th Floor, New York, NY 10006, USA

477 Williamstown Road, Port Melbourne, VIC 3207, Australia

314–321, 3rd Floor, Plot 3, Splendor Forum, Jasola District Centre,
New Delhi – 110025, India

103 Penang Road, #05–06/07, Visioncrest Commercial, Singapore 238467

Cambridge University Press is part of Cambridge University Press & Assessment,
a department of the University of Cambridge.

We share the University's mission to contribute to society through the pursuit of
education, learning and research at the highest international levels of excellence.

www.cambridge.org
Information on this title: www.cambridge.org/9781009499637

DOI: 10.1017/9781009499620

When citing this work, please include a reference to the DOI 10.1017/9781009499620

First published 2025

A catalogue record for this publication is available from the British Library

ISBN 978-1-009-49963-7 Hardback
ISBN 978-1-009-49965-1 Paperback
ISSN 2753-2674 (online)
ISSN 2753-2666 (print)

The Meaning of Constructions

Elements in Construction Grammar

DOI: 10.1017/9781009499620
First published online: May 2025

Benoît Leclercq
University of Lille

Cameron Morin
University of Paris-Cité

Author for correspondence: Benoît Leclercq, benoit.leclercq@univ-lille.fr

Abstract: This Element offers a primer for the study of meaning in a Construction Grammar approach. It reviews the main principles of meaning shared across constructionist frameworks, including its ubiquity in grammatical structure, its usage-based formation, and its nature as the output of cognitive representations. It also reviews the importance given to meaning in construction-based explanations of sentence composition, innovative language use, and language change. Paradoxically, the Element shows that there is no systematic framework delineating the rich structure of constructional meaning, which has led to theoretical disagreements and inconsistencies. It therefore proposes an operational model of meaning for practitioners of Construction Grammar. It details the characteristics of a complex interface of semantic, pragmatic, and social meaning, and shows how this framework sheds light on recent theoretical issues. The Element concludes by considering ways in which this framework can be used for future descriptive and theoretical research questions.

Keywords: Construction Grammar, meaning, semantics, pragmatics, sociolinguistics

ISBNs: 9781009499637 (HB), 9781009499651 (PB), 9781009499620 (OC)
ISSNs: 2753-2674 (online), 2753-2666 (print)

Contents

1 Introduction

> A focus on form to the neglect of function is like investigating a human organ such as the liver, without attending to what the liver does: while this is not impossible, it is certain to fail to be explanatory.
>
> Goldberg, *Constructions at Work: The Nature of Generalization in Language*

One of the foundational tenets of construction grammar (henceforth CxG) is that all linguistic forms are meaningful (Goldberg 2013: 16). In this Element, our main objective is to explore exactly what meaning is, how it materialises in language use, and how it should be modelled in a construction-based framework.

A number of key concepts will be introduced and critically discussed throughout the text. Some of them may be understood differently depending on the strand of CxG in which they are encountered (see Part II of Hoffmann and Trousdale 2013 for a detailed overview). Our approach is largely aligned with views developed in mainstream CxG (sometimes known as cognitive CxG, Boas 2013; Morin and Leclercq, in press). More generally, the framework we adopt is also compatible with the cognitive grammar approach of Langacker, who himself acknowledges that 'although the term had not yet been invented, the theory formulated was actually a kind of Construction Grammar' (Langacker 2005: 102). In addition, appropriate references to works from the broad approach of cognitive linguistics will be provided (Croft and Cruse 2004; Geeraerts and Cuyckens 2007).

As we address various issues in the constructionist approach to 'meaning', a number of underlying assumptions will guide our approach throughout. Although some of our readers (seasoned constructionists) may view these assumptions as basic, we wish to spell them out very explicitly. This is done to reach out to a wider readership (i.e., budding constructionists, students, or experienced linguists from other fields), as well as to ensure theoretical consistency, both in the overview that we present in the first half and the proposals that we make in the second half. In particular, assumptions about what constructions are exactly should be borne in mind throughout this Element. Goldberg (1995: 4, 2006: 5, 2019: 7) gave a number of technical definitions that have been critically discussed (Ungerer and Hartmann 2023: 5–11). A key point is that constructions are symbolic units, that is, form–meaning pairs. Though seemingly basic, this definition is not trivial, since CxG assumes that *all* linguistic knowledge consists of constructions: as in Goldberg's (2006: 18) famous words, 'it's constructions all the way down'. Behind this catchphrase lies one of CxG's most foundational design traits, namely, its non-modularity: there is no distinction between lexicon, syntax, and semantics, but they rather form an integrated whole. In this approach, language users possess only one repository of linguistic knowledge, the 'constructicon' (Jurafsky 1992). The constructicon is the repository of all existing constructions, which differ only in terms of complexity and schematicity (Croft and Cruse 2004: 255). To put it simply, the term 'construction' applies across the board to words, morphemes, idioms, and phrasal and clausal patterns. Crucially, all of these units are inherently meaningful. Furthermore, besides containing the entirety of linguistic knowledge, the constructicon is also assumed to take the shape of a structured network (see Diessel 2019a, 2023). As we will see, such a view has important implications for various aspects of constructional meaning.

The first part of this Element is meant as a primer on the meaning of constructions. Section 2 introduces the meaning-based assumption and aims to answer the question of what constructional meaning is. Section 3 then considers the question of how meaning is achieved in constructional use. The second aim of this Element is to provide a more advanced theoretical demonstration of how meaning should be modelled in CxG. It puts forward an explicit taxonomy of constructional meaning (Section 4.1); it explains how this taxonomy enables us to more adequately explain constructional variation (Section 4.2); and finally, it puts the limits of the constructicon to the test by considering the status of phonological knowledge (Section 4.3).

2 The Meaning-Based Assumption

2.1 Meaning Drives Grammar

Achieving an explicit model of meaning and its relationship with other aspects of language has always been a significant challenge in linguistics. For example, several accounts of the history of the field in the United States identify meaning as a major point of contention in the influential split between generative linguistics and cognitive linguistics originating in the 1970s (Harris 1993, 2022; Huck and Goldsmith 1996). The former approach, having gained increasing momentum over the 1950s and 1960s (Chomsky 1957, 1965), had put forward an 'interpretive' model of semantics. In this model, grammar was viewed as being essentially driven by an autonomous 'deep structure', which guided the interpretation of linguistic meaning in terms of objective truth conditions. Against and from within this popular model, former students and colleagues of Chomsky's, including George Lakoff, James McCawley, John Ross, and Paul Postal (Harris 2022), formulated an alternative approach known as generative semantics, which relied on what we will henceforth refer to as the 'meaning-based assumption': namely, the assumption that semantic structure is the true driver of grammar and linguistic knowledge. This meaning-based assumption came to be shared in the following years by an increasingly diverse family of functional approaches, many of which are now somewhat loosely subsumed under the label of 'cognitive linguistics' (Winter and Perek 2023), such as the theories of cognitive semantics (Talmy 2000), conceptual metaphor (Lakoff and Johnson 1980; Lakoff 1987), frame semantics (Fillmore 2006), cognitive grammar (Langacker 1987, 1991), and CxG (Hoffmann and Trousdale 2013): the theoretical framework we focus on in this Element.

Construction grammar, as a cognitive linguistic 'theory of syntax' (Croft and Cruse 2004: 4), is thus a meaning-based approach – indeed, as suggested by its historical context, a 'meaning-born' approach. First, it holds that all linguistic forms must be studied in their own right as inherently meaningful objects. 'Grammar does not involve any transformational or derivational component. Semantics is associated directly with surface form' (Goldberg 2013: 15). This is a crucial tenet in CxG which posits that any variation in form, as subtle as it may be, cannot simply be viewed as an unconstrained choice between variants of an underlying structure, but that each variant features its own set of idiosyncratic functional constraints (Goldberg 2002). A large body of work in CxG has thus investigated the topic of syntactic alternations to try and pin down the exact meaning contours of forms that were previously considered identical in the transformational accounts of generative grammar. Take, for instance, the DITRANSITIVE/*to*-DATIVE alternation (1) and the locative alternation (2).

(1) a. Mum gave her friend a present.
     b. Mum gave a present to her friend.

(2) a. The cook sprinkled the meat with salt.
     b. The cook sprinkled salt on the meat.

In both cases, the alternatives were long considered formal paraphrases or transformations from *a* to *b* where the propositions are taken to be identical (Chomsky 1957, 1965, 1971; Katz and Postal 1964). In CxG, the sentences in *a* and *b* involve different constructions that each express their own unique meaning. In (1), for instance, while the DITRANSITIVE construction (1a) and the *to*-DATIVE construction (1b) both express the notion of transfer (*X* CAUSES *Y* TO RECEIVE *Z*), the choice between these constructions is driven by a key semantic distinction. Namely, the *to*-DATIVE construction has been shown to iconically encode a greater conceptual distance between the agent (Mum) and the beneficiary (her friend) than the DITRANSITIVE construction (Thompson and Koide

1987: 400; Diessel 2019b: 71).[1] Similarly for the locative alternation (2), it has been demonstrated that the first alternative involves the *with*-APPLICATIVE construction, which encodes a holistic reading of the event (foregrounding the meat being fully covered in salt), while the second alternative involves the LOCATIVE CAUSED-MOTION construction, which encodes a partial reading of the event (foregrounding the action of the sprinkling, with only part of the meat being sprinkled) (Anderson 1971; Perek 2012).

Alternation studies of this type constitute 'a sizeable segment of the quantitative studies executed within construction-grammar' (Pijpops 2020: 283), and they are all the more significant in that they shed light on a range of other principles of linguistic knowledge and use. One of them is the 'principle of no synonymy' (Goldberg 1995: 67), recently reframed by Leclercq and Morin (2023) as the 'principle of no equivalence' (see Section 4.2), which basically states that any difference in form entails a difference in meaning. This principle captures the general observation that meaning is a crucial structuring force of linguistic knowledge. It also lays the ground for another essential cognitive process known as 'statistical preemption' (Goldberg 2019: 74), which refers to speakers' natural disposition 'not to use a formulation if an alternative formulation with the same function is consistently witnessed' (Boyd and Goldberg 2011: 55). As Leclercq and Morin (2023: 4) point out, 'while the principle of no synonymy posits that no two constructions have the exact same function, statistical preemption ensures that this be the case by blocking the use of an alternative (or new) form when a function is already associated with a specific construction'. This is why *stealer*, for instance, though a morphologically plausible construct of the V-*er* agentive construction, is blocked by the existing noun *thief* (Hoffmann 2022: 289), which already conventionally expresses the concept of 'a person taking something without the owner's permission'. Besides being a structuring force of linguistic knowledge, meaning is thus also a driving force of language use.

The specific issues considered in the preceding paragraphs illustrate the relevance of meaning applied to specific linguistic processes, but these applications are percolations from a more general and fundamental trait of language: that its 'primary function is to convey information' (Goldberg 2013: 16).[2]

---

[1] In fact, Goldberg (1995: 90) analyses *to*-DATIVE constructions as metaphorical extensions of CAUSED-MOTION constructions and considers that they express the meaning *X CAUSES Y TO MOVE TO Z* – a description which also captures the greater motion involved with the *to*-DATIVE construction.

[2] With this formulation, Goldberg could be taken to have fallen prey to the descriptive fallacy (Austin 1962: 3), whereby language only serves to make truth-evaluable statements. However, this is not the case, since Goldberg (2013: 16) explicitly adopts a broad acceptation of the term 'information' which applies to 'semantic or pragmatic (including information theoretic) distinctions'.

Meaning is thus at the heart of the constructional enterprise, to such an extent that from the oft-cited phrase that grammar is 'constructions all the way down' (Goldberg 2006: 18), we want to highlight the corollary that grammar is indeed *meaning* all the way down, given that all forms are symbolically associated with a specific meaning (thereby forming 'constructions'), and that this meaning motivates the use of these forms. Constructions, defined in CxG as the basic building blocks of language, emerge from our intersubjective communicational needs (Schmid 2020; Silvennoinen 2023), and these needs also explain the underlying processes involved in meaning variation and change (see Section 3.3).

2.2 Meaning Is Usage-Based

The meaning-based assumption of CxG is not just about the relationship between meaning and other aspects of language and grammar. It also concerns the nature of constructional meaning per se. As a non-modular approach to language, CxG assumes that meaning is acquired following the same principles as the rest of our linguistic knowledge. In this approach, linguistic knowledge is taken to be 'usage-based' and is described as directly emerging from language use (Bybee 2013; Perek 2023). It is the outcome of 'the cognitive organization of one's experience with language' (Bybee 2006a: 711), which Diessel (2019b: 51) defines as follows:'grammar is a dynamic system of emergent categories and flexible constraints that are always changing under the influence of domain-general cognitive processes involved in language use'. If, as argued in the previous section, grammar is inherently meaningful, it follows that meaning should also be viewed as a conceptual system that is dynamically shaped by usage. In this section, we highlight three major dimensions along which meaning is usage-based: first, it is emergent; second, it is experiential; and third, it is conventional.

2.2.1 Meaning Is Emergent

The first dimension pertains to processes of usage at play in the formation of meaning. According to usage-based theory, which CxG aligns with, each exposure to individual tokens of experience, known as 'exemplars' (Bybee 2010), leaves a memory trace in the mind of a language user (Goldberg 2019: 13). Although this memory trace includes any of the salient aspects of the original token of experience (see following paragraphs), it is considered 'lossy', in that not all details of the experience are retained (Goldberg 2019: 6). The first memory trace forms its own structured representation, against which memory traces of upcoming exemplars are analogically related in terms of (dis)similarity. Similar traces strengthen the initial representation and give rise to 'an EMERGENT CLUSTER (or "cloud"), which constitutes what we think of as a single coherent word meaning' (16).[3] Across contexts of use, constructions will tend to be associated with different clusters, thus forming their different (polysemous) meanings. These are constrained by two main structural principles: schematicity and prototypicality. The former, expounded by Langacker (2010), holds that besides retaining individual instances of use, processes of abstraction and generalisation also contribute to shaping the conceptual clusters and to forming new ones based on shared features (Goldberg 2006: 62). The latter posits that one of the clusters is construed as the 'prototypical' meaning of a construction given its particular conceptual centrality and cognitive salience (Mervis and Rosch 1981; Lakoff, 1987). As a consequence of these two principles, the meanings of constructions are assumed to be organised in structured networks of representation (Langacker 2010: 266; Lemmens 2016). Let us consider the following examples with the verb *run* (Figure 1).

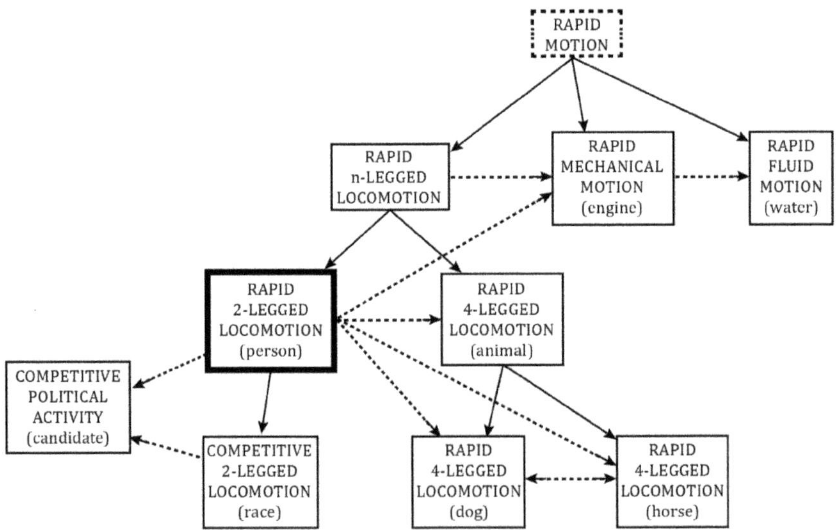

Figure 1 Conceptual network for the verb *run* (from Langacker 2010: 267).

---

[3] In CxG, the emergence of meanings as an outcome of usage is of course not limited to words, but applies to all constructions in general.

The representation in Figure 1 summarises a number of foundational aspects of the conceptual representations which the verb *run* is associated with. First, it is striking that the verb points to a multitude of related meanings (i.e., clusters), including 'rapid 2-legged locomotion' (e.g., *Evan ran the marathon in 3 hours*), 'rapid mechanical motion' (e.g., *This car runs at 200 mph*) or 'competitive political activity' (e.g., *Why did Tom choose to run for mayor?*). Second, it is notable that these meaning clusters are not listed as unrelated dictionary entries in our minds, but are interconnected and structured both by schematicity and prototypicality. Relations of schematicity are represented by the solid arrows. So for instance, the highest cluster, 'rapid motion', schematises the features that are shared by all the other clusters in the network. Prototype effects are captured by the box in bold, with broken arrows representing conceptual extensions from the prototype.

This specific example focuses on a network of word meanings, but given the continuity from lexicon to syntax assumed in CxG, schematicity and prototypicality also characterise networks of grammatical constructions. For example, Goldberg (1995: 38) showcases the role of prototypicality in shaping the network of meanings associated with the English DITRANSITIVE construction (SUBJ V OBJ1 OBJ2, see Example (1a)). She shows that a variety of meaning clusters radiates from the prototypical centre 'agent successfully causes recipient to receive patient' (e.g., *She fed the cat some fish*), including, for instance, the extensions 'agent causes recipient not to receive patient' (e.g., *My brother's boss denied him a pay raise*) and 'agent intends to cause recipient to receive patient' (e.g., *Dad knitted me a jumper*).

Regardless of the type of construction involved, it is crucial that the general process of concept formation described in this section is viewed as being constantly regulated by frequency effects in experience (Bybee 2013). Two main frequency effects that are commonly discussed are token frequency and type frequency (Kapatsinski 2023), which have an impact on cognitive entrenchment, levels of schematicity, and ease of activation and processing (Diessel 2007; Schmid 2012).

2.2.2 Meaning Is Experiential

The first dimension accounts for the way meaning comes about in the speaker's mind, that is, via emergent processes. We now turn to the second dimension, which accounts for the content of the meaning clusters. Because meaning emerges through exposure to individual usage events, it follows that the content of the meaning clusters themselves is rooted in experience. This is why meaning can be described as experiential:

all facets of the experience witnessed in a usage event are in principle liable to becoming entrenched. A useful definition of 'experience' is provided by Johnson (1987: xvi): '"experience," then, is to be understood in a very rich, broad sense as including basic perceptual, motor-program, emotional, historical, social, and linguistic dimensions. ... Experience involves everything that makes us human – our bodily, social, linguistic, and intellectual being combined in complex interactions that make up our understanding of our world.' It follows that meaning is inseparable from the contexts from which it emerges. Similarly to its non-modular approach to the lexicon–syntax distinction, CxG does not distinguish between a purely 'linguistic' context-free meaning and encyclopaedic knowledge. Rather, it assumes that the meaning of constructions is inherently encyclopaedic and that constructions provide points of access to this encyclopaedic knowledge (Langacker 2008: 39; Goldberg 2019: 12; though see Section 3.1 for discussion). Such an approach is to be related to the assumption of embodied cognition taken by most cognitive linguistic frameworks (Evans 2012), including CxG, sometimes explicitly so (see Bergen and Chang 2013).

What is important to keep in mind here is that facets of experience are not entrenched as an unstructured 'grab bag' of knowledge (Lemmens 2017: 107), but on the contrary form a highly structured network of related conceptual nodes. On this view, for example, the noun *bear* provides a point of access to a rich, cross-modal network of nodes centred on the prototypical brown bear, specifying its shape and colour, the super-category 'animals' and 'hibernating mammals' to which it belongs, its preferred natural habitat, the customary activities of eating honey and fishing for salmon in which it engages, the potential danger it represents for humans in particular due to its speed and especially long and sharp claws, and many more. Again, the encyclopaedic nature of constructional meaning can be observed on all points of the lexicon–syntax cline. So, for instance, as discussed by Schmid (2014: 240), the more complex idiomatic expression *I love you* 'calls up a whole world of associations', including, but not limited to, typical situations of use ('romantic'), participants engaging in this social interaction ('lovers'), the specific type of emotion that it expresses ('deep affection'), and the stereotypical use of the expression in cultural products ('melodramatic movies' or 'commercial pop songs'). Likewise, the schematic grammatical construction of the Dɪᴛʀᴀɴsɪᴛɪᴠᴇ does not only signify the very highly abstract meaning of 'X ᴄᴀᴜsᴇs Y ᴛᴏ ʀᴇᴄᴇɪᴠᴇ Z' (cf. Goldberg 1995: 49), but it is also assumed to activate a rich network of knowledge relating to 'what a transfer actually involves, ... the respective roles of agents, recipients and themes and the relation between them, as well as who/what can usually perform these roles' (Leclercq 2024a: 20).

Other argument structure constructions (e.g., the Resultative, Causative, Locative) can be analysed along similar lines, with their meaning being inherently grounded in our basic experiences of events in the world (Hilpert 2019: 26–31). The major role of experience in the shaping and meaning of grammatical constructions is highlighted by Goldberg (1995: 39) in what she calls the 'scene encoding hypothesis' (see Kasper and Purschke 2023 for a recent discussion):

> *Scene Encoding Hypothesis*: constructions which correspond to basic sentence types encode as their central senses event types that are basic to human experience.

Finally, a notable implication of the experiential nature of meaning concerns the typological variability of constructions across languages (Goldberg 2013: 16): because the meaning of constructions is in large part motivated by non-linguistic experience, linguistic 'universals' are to be explained by similarities of experience across human cultures (in addition to domain-general cognitive constraints) rather than in terms of innate principles.

2.2.3 Meaning Is Conventional

Together, the two dimensions of constructional meaning described in Sections 2.2.1 and 2.2.2 lay stress on language as an entrenched cognitive system, where emergent and experiential processes are taken to affect the mind of an individual language user. However, these two dimensions do not provide a complete picture if we fail to take into account the third usage-based dimension, which accounts for the intersubjective functions that meaning fulfils: namely, that meaning is conventional. In his entrenchment-and-conventionalisation model, which is a cousin theory to CxG, Schmid (2020) makes explicit that one's knowledge of a language, including meaning, is not only the result of cognitive processes of entrenchment. It also importantly relies on social processes of conventionalisation, driven by the interpersonal needs for mutual understanding and shared intentionality at the heart of communication. Although CxG is also underpinned by this assumption, sometimes explicitly so (Croft 2009; Goldberg 2013; Traugott and Trousdale 2013), it has generally been underappreciated. In a recent discussion, though, Silvennoinen (2023: 1) specifically pleads for a strong view of constructions as 'social conventions that function as intersubjective cues for meaning'. In other words, the formation of meaning is not viewed as yielding unconstrained aggregates of experience, but as being notably regulated in usage by the intersubjective functions of language. The usage-based nature of meaning is thus also manifest in the way in which it shapes language at the level of the community: for example, it explains why communal languages consistently emerge in spite of idiolectal variation (Beckner et al. 2009). Our present approach aligns with these recent concerns and we consider convention to play an essential role in the construction of meaning.

2.3 Meaning Is Construal

In the previous section, we delineated the main usage-based factors giving rise to meaning in the individual mind and in the community. We now turn to a synchronic overview of the end-point of these processes: what is meaning? Although this question will also be the focus of our theoretical proposals in Section 4, here we review the constructionist assumptions commonly adopted to address it.

The usage-based approach of CxG already echoes two notable hypotheses on the nature of meaning. First, its emergent and experiential origins are taken to refute the traditional Aristotelian or 'classical' framework of meaning as a list of necessary and sufficient binary conditions (also known as componential, definitional, or feature list analysis; see Geeraerts 2010 and Riemer 2010). Rather, meaning is made up of clusters of experience subject to prototype effects. Second, these usage-based origins are taken to refute the view that meaning involves (combinations of) innate and/or atomic conceptual primitives (Lakoff 1987: 166; Evans and Green 2006: 208). Instead, meaning consists in a rich network of encyclopaedic knowledge.

Another dimension of meaning that is often discussed concerns the relationship between language and the world. Many traditional approaches in philosophy of language view this relationship as one where linguistic meaning is ultimately determined by the conditions under which it is true or false, that is, its truth conditions with respect to states of affairs in the world (see Carston 2010 for an overview). This approach 'takes the language–world relation as the basic concern of semantics rather than the language–mind relation' (Carston 2010: 280). Construction grammar rejects this approach. Instead, it contends that 'meanings are in the head' (Gärdenfors 1999: 21) and therefore takes the language–mind relation as basic (though see Section 4.2 for a careful discussion). Such an assumption is shared with cognitive linguistics more generally. In particular, it is assumed that our conceptual knowledge is best approached in terms of the construals that the mind derives from experience. The notion of construal has been operationalised in different ways, often discussed in terms of frames (Fillmore 1985), idealised cognitive models (Lakoff 1987), and domains (Langacker 1987). The term 'frames' is most common in CxG research, as illustrated in the growing domain of constructicography (Lyngfelt et al. 2018, Boas 2021, in press); however, it should be noted that idealised cognitive models and domains are alternative terms that are considered to be 'often interchangeable' (Langacker 2008: 46). Fillmore defines a frame as follows:

> By the term 'frame' I have in mind any system of concepts related in such a way that to understand any one of them you have to understand the whole structure in which it fits; when one of the things in such a structure is introduced into a text, or into a conversation, all of the others are automatically made available. (Fillmore 1982: 373)

Consider the example of the lexical construction *waiter*. The concept associated with this word can only be interpreted in relation to other concepts in the same frame, such as 'occupation', 'restaurant' or 'bar', 'customer', 'ordering', 'serving', 'menu' and so forth. Similarly, Lemmens (2016: 92) shows that the construction *school night* can only be understood within a larger frame that comprises (sociocultural) knowledge about what constitutes a 'day', a 'week', a 'weekend', a 'school day', 'school', 'sleep patterns', 'time management' and so forth. The notion of frame extends to more grammatical constructions as well. It is, for instance, used by Goldberg (1995: 142–151) to describe the meaning of the DITRANSITIVE construction. While it is typically described as encoding '*Agent* CAUSE-RECEIVE *Recipient Theme*', Goldberg specifically argues that the meaning of the construction is more complex than these conceptual primitives. Notably, the full knowledge of the DITRANSITIVE includes rich information regarding both the event and the arguments, viewed as involving a 'successful act of transfer', a 'volitive' agent, and a 'willing' recipient. Boas (2021: 51) also points out that the construction 'evoke[s] the GIVING frame', comprising knowledge of 'ownership', 'loss of possession', 'intentionality', 'offering', 'permanence' and so forth.[4]

These examples show that a construction foregrounds one element of a frame, typically called the 'figure', which is understood against the rest of the backgrounded conceptual frame, typically called the 'ground'. This part–whole relationship characterising the meaning of a construction (Diessel 2019a: 95) is foundational to the notion of construal introduced in the previous paragraphs. To illustrate this, Diessel discusses the distinction between the verbal constructions *send* and *receive*.[5] They both evoke the TRANSFER frame, but

---

[4] See the entry 'Giving' in FrameNet at https://framenet2.icsi.berkeley.edu/fnReports/data/frame/Giving.xml. Last accessed 18 December 2023.

[5] An earlier illustration can be found in Goldberg (1995), who shows that the difference between the apparently synonymous verbs *rob* and *steal* depends on which participants of the <thief target goods> frame are being profiled. 'In the case of *rob*, the target and the thief are profiled while in the case of *steal* the valuables and the thief are profiled' (Goldberg 1995: 45).

they foreground two different elements of this frame: *send* foregrounds the agent and *receive* foregrounds the recipient. They thus profile two distinct figures in a single frame, and which verb the speaker will choose depends on their vantage point on the situation (see also Langacker 2008: 76 for a similar analysis of the prepositions *in front of* and *behind*). Conversely, a single element can be construed as the figure in distinct frames. For example, the concept of the 'dry surface of the earth' (Fillmore 1982: 121) can be equally foregrounded by the nouns *land* and *ground*, though the former is couched in the maritime frame (as in (3)) while the latter is couched in the aerial frame (as in (4)).

(3)   [This type of bird] spends its life on land. (Fillmore 1982: 121)

(4)   [This type of bird] spends its life on the ground. (Fillmore 1982: 121)

Again, the figure–ground distinction is a structuring principle of grammatical meaning by the same token as lexical meaning. It enables us to explain a range of phenomena pertaining to constructional alternations (introduced in Section 2.1) where two different syntactic constructions offer distinct construals. An obvious instance of this is the active/passive alternation.

Both of these constructions activate the frame of transitive actions, which typically represent an 'agent' acting upon either a 'patient' (in the case of transitives) or a 'theme' and its 'recipient' (in the case of ditransitives). Which of the active or the passive voice is used depends, among other factors, on which of the participants is construed as the figure (Divjak, Millin, and Medimorec 2020). In the most canonical case of the agent being construed as the figure, the active construction is used (5). Conversely, if the foregrounded element is the patient (6a and b) or the theme (6c), the passive construction is used, backgrounding the agent and sometimes even omitting it.

(5)   a. Tom sent me an email this morning.
       b. The baby woke me up.

(6)   a. I was sent an email this morning.
       b. An email was sent to me this morning.
       c. I was woken up by the baby.

The notion of construal, operationalised here in frame-semantic terms, is at the heart of the constructionist approach to meaning. In the literature, other key concepts are typically discussed alongside this notion. The most notable ones include conceptual metaphor (Lakoff and Johnson 1980), mental spaces (Fauconnier 1994; Fauconnier and Turner 2008), and force dynamics (Talmy 1988). The first two are discussed further in Section 3. But here, we want to focus briefly on metaphors and metonymy. According to Lakoff (1993), metaphors are conceptual phenomena that consist in mapping two distinct domains (or frames). These domains are organised in an asymmetrical relationship where one of the domains (the source) is used to construe the other (the target). A classic example is the conceptual metaphor LOVE IS A JOURNEY. As shown in Evans and Green (2006: 295), this conceptual metaphor involves a complex range of mappings between a source and a target, which licence a number of metaphorical expressions foregrounding different figures across domains. For instance, 'LOVERS become TRAVELLERS (*We're at a crossroads*), who travel by a particular MEANS OF TRANSPORT (*We're spinning our wheels*), proceeding along a particular ROUTE (*Our relationship went off course*), impeded by obstacles (*Our marriage is on the rocks*)' (Evans and Green 2006: 295).

Metonymy is a related phenomenon, but instead of construing a domain in terms of another unrelated domain, it identifies one element (the vehicle) of a specific domain as standing for some other element (the target) of the same or a contiguous domain (Evans and Green 2006: 315; Kövecses, 2006: 99). The vehicle thus provides a (salient) point of access to the target within a particular domain (Littlemore 2015: 5). Common conceptual metonymic patterns include PART FOR WHOLE, CONTAINER FOR CONTENT, and PRODUCER FOR PRODUCT, respectively instantiated in (7) to (9). In (7), *butt* stands for 'self'; in (8), *kettle* stands for 'water'; and in (9) *Cadillac* stands for 'car'.

(7)   Get your *butt* over here.

(8)   The *kettle* is boiling!

(9)   He dumped the bags in the *Cadillac*.

In CxG, as in cognitive linguistics more generally, it is assumed that conceptual metaphors and metonymy are pervasive in language and thought, and constitute one of the key sources of polysemy (Lakoff 1988: 39). That is, although they provide templates that shape our conceptual reasoning, their repeated use in language leads to the conventionalisation of linguistic metaphors and metonymies. Importantly, their basic unit is the domain, which corresponds to the notion of 'frame' discussed in this section (Kövecses, 2006: 99; Littlemore, 2015: 9–10). These processes evince the central role of frames for our understanding of the nature of linguistic meaning (Willich 2022).

2.4 Summary

In this section, we presented and unpacked the meaning-based assumption at the heart of CxG. This assumption was shown to be made up of five core components. First, meaning drives grammar. It occupies a central, generative role in the language system and can by no means be separated from linguistic form. In fact, CxG as a theory of syntax can be described as meaning-focused. Second, meaning is usage-based. As the label suggests, the use of language is the primary arena where meaning is formed. We broke down this component into three subcomponents: (i) meaning is emergent because it relies on repeated usage; (ii) meaning is experiential because it is a record of usage contexts; and (iii) meaning is conventional because language use is a social practice. Finally, meaning is construal. It is a cognitive representation of experience in the human mind rather than a direct model of reality.

Together, these components provide a principled explanation of what the meaning of constructions consists of. Having established this, the next step in our account is to answer the following question: how is meaning dynamically constructed and negotiated in the use of language? We consider this question in the next section.

3 Meaning in Use

3.1 The Construction of Meaning

Answering the question of what it means to 'mean' depends not only on what material constructions make available to language users, but also on how the latter draw on this material in language use. A central assumption in CxG is that the constructions we use do not point towards purely 'linguistic', context-free, static concepts (see Section 2.2.2). Rather, the interpretation of constructions is assumed to involve a dynamic process of meaning construction (Diessel 2019a: 27–30). So constructions are viewed as providing cues or 'points of access' (Langacker 2008: 39; Goldberg 2019: 12) to an array of encyclopaedic information which constitutes a construction's *meaning potential* (Leclercq 2023a: 337). For this reason, Langacker (2008: 30) favours the term *conceptualisation* to that of *concept* when referring to the construction of meaning.

The view of meaning as conceptualisation is not unique to CxG, but is shared with most frameworks in cognitive linguistics (Evans and Green 2006). It ties in with the usage-based assumption discussed in Section 2.2, whereby meaning emerges from individual usage events. However, outside of the cognitive linguistic literature, it may not be clear what 'conceptualisation' involves exactly. Conceptualisation is a process which, at its core, is often equated with the cognitive phenomenon of 'activation' (Langacker 2008: 42; Evans 2006: 520; Bergen 2016: 143). To put it simply, different parts of the conceptual network associated with a construction will be cognitively highlighted, to a greater or lesser degree, depending on a number of contextual factors, including levels of entrenchment and salience, previous discourse context, the current speech event, as well as considerations of the physical and sociocultural context. The dynamicity of conceptualisation is evinced by its inherent variability, to the extent that 'an expression appears to have different values on different occasions [and] is never used twice with exactly the same meaning' (Langacker 2008: 50). Consider the lexical item *watch* used in the examples below, from Dawson and Phelan (2016: 481):

(10) A frantic-looking man runs up to a group of people standing at a bus stop, checks the bus schedule, and then says hurriedly, 'Do any of you have a watch?'

(11) Your linguistics instructor left his watch at home this morning, but he will need to monitor his time use in class. He wanders into the department lounge and says to his colleagues, 'Do any of you have a watch?'

(12) A group of preteen girls is comparing jewelry. One girl says, 'My jewelry is best, because I have the most.' Another says, 'Nope. Mine is the best because it all matches.' This sort of thing goes on for a while. Finally the last girl pipes up that she thinks she has the best jewelry. 'Oh yeah? What makes you so special?' She replics, 'Just look at my wrist! Do any of you have a watch?'

(13) A mugger traps a group of people in a dark alley and waves a gun at them while screaming, 'Do any of you have a watch?'

In (10), the particular aspect activated in the conceptual network of 'watch' is its function to tell the time. Example (11) highlights the nature of 'watch' as a physical object that can be lent from its owner to someone else. In (12), the facet of 'watch' that is activated is its social value as a fashionable piece of jewellery. Finally, (13) activates the economic value that watches may have as goods prone to be coveted by thieves. All four examples thus represent distinct conceptualisations of a single conceptual frame. In addition, these examples also illustrate distinct conceptualisations at the grammatical level, namely the speech acts achieved by interrogative constructions, such as the one used in 'Do any of you have a watch?'. In all cases, the interrogative serves as a request, but (10) activates a request for information (i.e., to know the time); (11) activates a request for action (i.e., to lend a watch); (12) activates a *false* request (as a rhetorical question) for a specific predetermined answer (here, the negative); and (13) activates a unilateral command.

While the process of activation plays a crucial underlying role in conceptualisation, a number of other processes are important to take into account as well. For example, as explained in Section 2.3, conceptual metaphors and metonymies are ubiquitous aspects of conceptual knowledge, and they are thus also important to consider in a dynamic, conceptualisation perspective. Importantly, conceptual metaphors and metonymies are not just static mappings but also specific effects of activation. For instance, the interpretation of the noun *roof* in *Prices are going through the roof* involves the co-activation of the concept 'roof' and the conceptual metaphor MORE IS UP (Desagulier and Monneret 2023: 36). Likewise, the interpretation of the noun *hoover* as 'vacuum cleaner' in *She took out the hoover* involves the co-activation of the concept 'hoover' and the conceptual metonymies PRODUCER FOR PRODUCT and MEMBER OF A CATEGORY FOR A CATEGORY (Littlemore 2015: 32). In addition, these auxiliary processes do not necessarily occur in isolation but are also prone to occur together, for instance in what Goossens (1990) calls 'metaphtonymies'. A case in point is the adjective *close-lipped* (Goossens 1990: 332), such as in the sentence *[Nick Faldo]'s always been a favorite of mine, but famously close-lipped with the press* (Davies 2008-). Here, we can either interpret the adjective *close-lipped* as meaning 'who does not talk much' or 'who talks in a way that does not reveal much'. While the first interpretation only involves the metonymy BODY PART FOR FUNCTION, the second activates both that metonymy and the metaphor DISCRETION IS SILENCE.

Conceptualization is also the focus of a related cognitive linguistic framework known as blending theory (stemming from the theory of mental spaces, Fauconnier 1994, 1997; Fauconnier and Turner 1998, 2008), which is often compared with conceptual metaphor theory (see Grady, Oakley and Coulson 1999 and Evans and Green 2006: 400–444 for an overview). As the name suggests, blending theory aims to describe the phenomenon of conceptual 'blends' in on-line conceptualisation. Blends emerge as the result of a dynamic integration combining input mental spaces in language use, the latter being 'temporary conceptual domains constructed during ongoing discourse' (Evans and Green 2006: 371). When these input spaces recruit distinct frames with an asymmetrical projection from one to the other, the integration results in a metaphorical interpretation. By contrast, when the input spaces recruit related frames in such a projection, the integration results in a metonymic interpretation. An important contribution of blending theory to conceptual metaphor theory is that such conceptual integrations typically result in more than the sum of their parts, with emergent properties adding some unique conceptual information as a by-product of network integration. In the sentence *That surgeon is a butcher* (Evans and Green 2006: 401), for instance, the conceptualisation foregrounds a notion of incompetence which is not inherent to either of the frames SURGEON or BUTCHER, but rather has emerged from the perceived incompatibility of the skills of a butcher for the tasks entrusted to a surgeon. Besides blends constructed on the fly at the lexical level, Turner (1991) shows that grammatical constructions can project lexical words directly onto the blended space as a result of their conventional meaning. An illustrative case is the XYZ construction, which one can find in sentences like *Children are the riches of poor men* (Turner 1991: 199). This construction prompts a conceptual blend where the emergent property is a conjunction between the relations X–Z (e.g., *children–poor men*) and Y–W (e.g., *riches–rich men*), where W is a recruited frame element related to Y. Importantly, the conjunction exists in neither of the three input spaces of X, Y and Z. Such blends that are prompted by particular constructions are called 'formal blends'. They show that blending is relevant not only for describing conceptual structure and linguistic meaning alone, but also for describing grammatical composition. Indeed, Fauconnier and Turner (1996) argue that blending is 'a central process of grammar' and view grammatical constructions as conventional blends.

Recent research in CxG has picked up on the insights of blending theory to develop new perspectives on the topic of grammatical composition per se. Hoffmann (in press: 6), for instance, argues that it 'can best account for constructional combination'. Setting aside questions of blending and its relation to creative language use, we now turn to a thorny issue that needs to be addressed, namely constructional combination and compositionality. The construction of meaning is indeed not only the preserve of individual constructions but also takes place as a result of the generative power of grammar. Much like 'it is clear that language is not a set of sentences that can be fixed in advance' (Goldberg 2006: 22), it is equally clear that the meaning of sentences cannot be established in advance either. The traditional approach to the interpretation of sentences relies on the concept of compositionality, which posits that the meaning of the whole sentence derives from the functions of its constituent parts (Partee 1995). Rambelli (2025) aptly notes that in this regard CxG could be perceived as taking issue with this concept, given that – beside the lexical level – language users are argued to know a wide variety of more complex constructions that may show features of idiomaticity (i.e., non-compositionality). However, we want to stress that the tendency for many constructions to have non-compositional meaning does *not* entail that CxG negates compositionality. As Kay and Michaelis (2019: 293) point out, 'it is sometimes supposed that constructional approaches are opposed to compositional semantics. This happens to be an incorrect supposition.' Quite the contrary, compositionality is an essential trait of constructional use, as evinced by the distinction in the CxG literature between the *construction* and the *construct*. While the former term refers to entrenched and conventional signs, the latter term refers to 'a single token of performance that is the result of construction interaction' (Hoffmann 2022: 4). In other words, actual use of language inevitably results in the combination of different constructions, the interpretation of which cannot but involve a compositional process. Take, for instance, the representation of the sentence

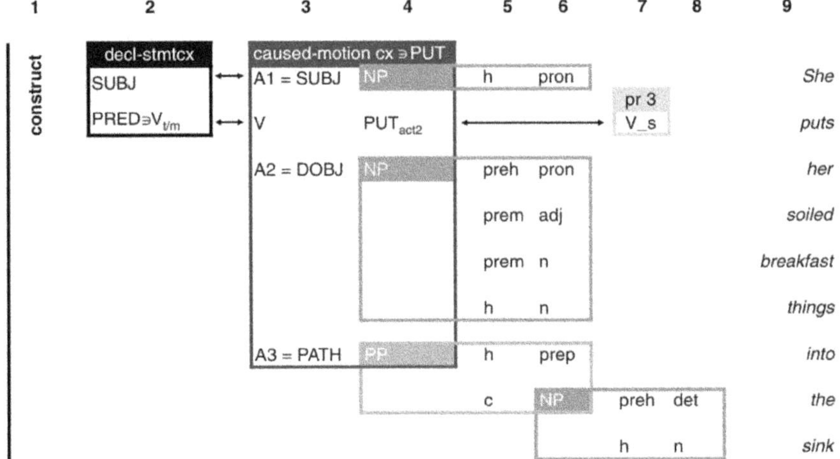

Figure 2 Construction grid for *She puts her soiled breakfast things into the sink* (from Herbst and Hoffmann 2018: 201).

She puts her soiled breakfast things into the sink using the annotation framework of the constructional approach to syntactic analysis (CASA, Herbst and Hoffmann 2018, 2024), detailed in Figure 2.

Figure 2 shows that an authentic token of language use (the construct) results from a complex, hierarchical combination of a variety of constructions. In other words, CxG adopts a view of compositionality that is not restricted to the lexical level. Compositional meaning emerges from the way that constructions are combined. In the case at hand, this means that the interpretation of the sentence *She puts her soiled breakfast things into the sink* depends not only on the individual words used (listed in column 9) but also on the function of the different constructions in which they appear, including the Noun and Preposition Phrase constructions (columns 4–6), the Caused-Motion construction (columns 3–4), and the more general Declarative-'Statement' construction (column 2). Of course, the breakdown of this sentence does not unilaterally exclude the possibility for non-compositional meaning to play a role in sentence processing. Note that the meaning features of this sentence are not specified in Figure 2 and that, for example, there may well be some aspect of the meaning of the Caused-Motion construction that is non-compositional (Goldberg 1995: 165). Overall, what the example goes to show is that CxG does not categorically choose non-compositionality over compositionality (or vice-versa) in its theoretical explanations; rather, it allows for both to exist and models their complementary roles in language processing.[6]

---

[6] Another phenomenon modelled by CxG which further underlines the role of compositionality in the language network is that of 'multiple inheritance' (Croft 2001: 26; Hilpert 2019: 63–65; see

Compositionality is classically understood as a feature of the interpreting process of language. In CxG, this feature is also an integral part of language production. Meaning construction is thus two-pronged: it is a central process both for the hearer interpreting a construct *and* for the speaker producing a construct. More than this, the interpretation of an utterance depends on how it has been constructed by a speaker before it is eventually processed by the hearer. This speaker-initiated process is viewed as generative in that compositionality allows for a wide range of more or less novel constructs to be produced. At the same time, the generative power of language is constrained, not only because speakers have finite linguistic means, but also because there are a number of specific cognitive principles that limit the range of possible constructs.

In her seminal book, Goldberg (1995: 50) introduced two such principles, namely the semantic coherence principle and the correspondence principle, which apply to argument structure constructions in particular. The first of these predicts that combined constructions should feature compatible semantic roles. Goldberg (1995: 51) gives the example of the verb *hand*, which she argues readily appears in the Ditransitive construction because the participant roles of 'hander', 'handee' and 'handed' fuse unproblematically with the 'agent', 'recipient' and 'patient' argument roles of the ditransitive (e.g., *The postman handed me a letter*). By contrast, the second principle predicts that each profiled participant role of a lexical frame must be fused with an argument role of the argument structure construction. This explains why *Paul handed a letter* and *Paul handed the postman* are unacceptable constructs, for the handing frame includes obligatory profiled 'recipient' and 'patient' roles which are absent from the Transitive argument structure construction.

In the CxG literature, a range of other, more broadly cognitive principles have been studied as pressures on linguistic structure and meaning composition. One of them is *statistical pre-emption*, a notion we introduced in Section 2.1. Statistical pre-emption offers a usage-based explanation for the observation that speakers will refrain from uttering constructs whose intended meaning is already expressed by an existing construction. This is for instance why speakers of English will prefer to use the irregular past form *went* to the regular form *goed*. For the same reason, speakers will prefer using the adjective *asleep* in

---

Sommerer 2020 for an overview and discussion). According to this notion, the structure of a construction can be (and often is) described as an assembly which inherits its component parts from higher-level constructions. So not only are utterances the direct result of compositionality, but the building blocks of these utterances (i.e., constructions) often inherit their properties from other constructions themselves. We will not discuss the notion of multiple inheritance in detail in this book (perhaps unfortunately; see Sommerer 2020).

a predicative position (*The child is asleep*) rather than in an attributive position (*The asleep child*), and the verb *explain* in the *to*-Dative construction (*Explain this to me*) rather than in the Ditransitive construction (*Explain me this*). In other words, speakers' construction of meaning is also largely determined by what they consistently witness and what they 'learn not to say' (Boyd and Goldberg, 2011: 80).

Statistical pre-emption is an important factor for understanding a more general feature of composition, namely 'productivity' (Barðdal 2008, Traugott and Trousdale 2013, Goldberg 2019). The notion of productivity refers to the extensibility of a constructional schema, that is, the speaker's ability to use novel lexical items in a schematic construction (Barðdal 2008: 53). For instance, the sentence *He cheated his way into the Olympics* reflects a productive use of the Way construction (Subj$_i$ V Pron$_i$'s *way* Obl; Israel 1996) which here is creatively extended to the verb *cheat* (see Section 3.2 for more details on creativity). Importantly, productivity is not categorical but is measured on a cline, with some constructions being more productive than others, and the majority of constructional schemas are in fact only partially productive (Goldberg 2019: 62). This entails that speakers are not at full liberty to come up with any new combinations when they construct meaning. In CxG, two important factors have been shown to have an impact on productivity: statistical pre-emption and coverage. Specifically, Goldberg (2016: 373) argues that productivity is constrained by statistical pre-emption and encouraged by high degrees of coverage. On the one hand, statistical pre-emption restricts productivity as certain combinations may be blocked by other existing conventions in the language. On the other hand, coverage is said to encourage productive uses of a construction (i.e., coinages) if the subsequent representation of the construction (updated by the coinage) is sufficiently similar to the speaker's initial representation of that construction. Coverage is a multifactorial feature that depends on the well-established properties of type frequency, semantic/ phonological variability, and similarity between coinage and attested exemplars (Goldberg 2019: 63). We will focus on examples (14) to (16) to illustrate this notion.

(14)   I might just go up town and track down a chestnut cart and get a chance to *scald* the hell out of my tongue. (Davies 2008-)

(15)   I'm going to *hug* the hell out of you. (Davies 2008-)

(16)   ?He *called* the hell out of his brother.

All of these examples instantiate the 'V *the hell out of* NP' construction (Perek 2016). In (14), the use of *scald* in verbal position is fully acceptable because its meaning as an instance of 'physical injury' corresponds to the 'most dense [verb] class' (which displays high type frequency and low semantic variability) associated with the construction (Goldberg 2019: 67). In other words, coverage is high and the coinage is easily sanctioned given the similarity between the coinage and previous exemplars. In (15), the use of *hug* in this construction comes across as more marginal (and perhaps odd). This is because the class of physical verbs with a 'weaker' force appears to be sparser (low type frequency and high semantic variability), and there is less similarity between the use of this verb and other attested exemplars. So coverage is relatively lower and the coinage is not so easily sanctioned. Finally, (16) showcases a fictitious example of a candidate coinage that is unlikely to be sanctioned. This is because the verb *call* belongs to none of the four main verb classes identified by Perek (2016) for the construction (namely, psych verbs, abstract actions, forceful physical actions, and weaker physical actions). Coverage is therefore especially low, and the coinage improbable. What all of the preceding observations illustrate is that, as they construct sentences trying to convey meaning, speakers are also guided by a number of cognitive pressures that circumscribe the set of potential coinages.

The last question we want to address is how to establish exactly what the cognitive underpinnings of all the processes identified in this section are. That is, what makes conceptualisation, metaphor, metonymy, blending, and composition possible? As mentioned in the previous paragraphs, it is typically assumed that the meaning of an expression depends on the degree to which elements of a conceptual network are activated. The notion of activation is most prevalent in Langacker's work, but it also appears to be central across cognitive linguistic frameworks. Activation is mainly discussed in relation to lexical conceptualizations, although we have seen that it can reasonably be extended to grammatical constructions as well. In addition, activation is traditionally completed by the process of analogy, a type of similarity-based reasoning, which is viewed as particularly foundational to the integration of constructions through composition (Rambelli 2025). For instance, the notions of coverage and productivity introduced earlier directly hinge on analogy, as they rest upon similarity judgements. Likewise, blending is often likened to a process of analogical mapping (Fauconnier 2001). More generally, analogy is so central to usage-based models that its iterative nature is said to lay the foundation of grammatical competence (Glynn 2022). However, activation and analogy alone do not exhaust the full range of processes involved. It is also assumed that these processes are completed by contextual, inferential processes in order to capture the speaker's intended meaning. Inference, for instance, is identified as one of the key components of blending (Fauconnier and Turner 1998), especially in accounts of emergent structure in conceptual blends (see the inference of incompetence triggered by the surgeon/butcher blend). Inference is of course also recognised as playing a central role in the derivation of many kinds of fully contextual components of meaning, such as conversational implicatures or indirect speech acts, even though they have not garnered sustained focus in CxG. By contrast, Leclercq (2024a: 108) has recently argued that besides processes of activation and analogy, CxG should also systematically integrate inferential processes among the key factors needed to determine the explicit content of an expression, regardless of how creative it is. The idea that conceptualisation involves the enrichment of input information via inference is echoed in research in the field of vision and gestalt psychology (e.g., Lehar 2002) and appears to have inspired initial developments in cognitive semantics (Diessel 2019a: 28). Attention to the role of inference in meaning construction thus cannot be minimised.

3.2 Functional Innovations

Section 3.1 identified meaning construction from the viewpoint of what the linguistic system allows speakers to do. To complete our account, we turn to the question of whether and how speakers can depart from the possibilities offered by the system when making meaning.

One of the earliest phenomena discussed in CxG research is 'coercion'. This phenomenon is directly linked to the notion of productivity, which we introduced earlier as the speaker's capacity to extend existing constructions to new lexical items. There are naturally cases where the new lexical item will readily appear in the construction, such as the verb *swing* in the WAY construction as illustrated in (17).

(17) Regardless, that didn't stop you guys coming out in full force to share your thoughts on this controversial topic and it's clear that you believe it will still be Peter Parker *swinging* his way around New York with a new costume and darker attitude. (Davies 2008-)

This construct succeeds in combining the WAY construction and a new lexical item in a relatively inconspicuous way because of two main factors: not only is the WAY construction highly productive (as shown, for instance, by the very high number of hapax legomena found in the Corpus of Contemporary American English), but the core meaning of *swing* in fact matches the 'manner of motion' semantics of the argument structure construction. Not all extensions feature such a clean match between the schema and the item, though, and language use is also rife with apparent mismatches. It is these types of cases that are most clearly under the purview of coercion. Coercion indeed occurs in case of a semantic mismatch between a lexical item and its morphosyntactic context. The following examples are cases in point:

(18) He *sneezed* the napkin off the table. (Goldberg 1995: 9)

(19) Three *beers* please! (Hilpert 2019: 17)

(20) That was so un-*gucci*. (Hoffmann 2022: 51)

(21) Not to beat a dead horse, but it would appear that the *wokes* are in an abusive relationship with the speech policemen, given that some of their favored terms are being abruptly disallowed (like trigger warning or 'preferred' pronouns).[7]

(22) I just *Google Mapped* my way to an exam because I didn't know where Engineering South was. #senior year (Leclercq 2024a: 30)

(23) I didn't like how he '*what-abouted*' the shooting as if we can't do anything about the gun violence and we should learn to accept it. (X)[8]

The example in (18) showcases the now classic example of the intransitive verb *sneeze* used in the CAUSED-MOTION construction. In principle, *sneeze* does not select a patient argument in its semantics, let alone an oblique argument, and therefore would not be expected to occur in a transitive argument structure construction. Its interpretation in (18) is coerced by the CAUSED-MOTION construction. In (19), the noun *beer,* which is most typically encountered as uncountable, is used in two individuating constructions (namely, *three* N_{count} and N_{count}-*s*), which force an interpretation of *beer* as a countable noun, whereby the speaker is understood as requesting three portions of beer (e.g., glasses or bottles). In (20), the proper noun *Gucci* is used in a morphological schema in which the prefix *un-* typically selects an adjective. There is both a semantic and morphosyntactic mismatch, since *Gucci* is commonly used to refer to a brand rather than to depict particular attributes, and so takes the form of a noun. Its use in the *un-*ADJ construction guides us towards an adjectival interpretation. Conversely, example (21) shows that an adjective (*woke*) can also receive a nominal interpretation when used in constructions that select a nominal head (such as the DEFINITE DETERMINATION and the PLURAL constructions). Likewise, the denominal verb *Google Mapped* in (22) results from the use of a noun referring to a navigating app as a manner-of-motion verb in the WAY construction. Finally, a slightly less discussed but equally relevant type of coercion can be found in (23). In this case, it is the lexically specific elements

---

[7] From: https://www.nationalreview.com/corner/you-cant-say-that-at-stanford/. Last accessed 26 February 2024.

[8] From: https://twitter.com/DavidSp43256698/status/1747008007546790330. Last accessed 26 February 2024.

'what about' from the idiomatic construction *What about* X?, a rhetorical question aimed to index the speaker's annoyance and dismiss the interlocutor's argument, that are used as a verb in the TRANSITIVE construction through the use of the 'phrase as lemma construction' (Goldberg and Shirtz in press).[9] In all of these examples, the interpretation is argued to take place in accordance with the following principle:

> *The override principle*. If a lexical item is semantically incompatible with its morphosyntactic context, the meaning of the lexical item conforms to the meaning of the structure in which it is embedded. (Michaelis 2004: 25)

In keeping with this principle, the lexically specific constructions *sneeze*, *beer*, *gucci*, *woke*, *Google Map*, and *what about* were interpreted in accordance with the meaning of the more schematic constructions in which they were used. So there is coercion in these examples, in the sense that the meaning of those lexemes is largely inherited from the constructions in which they occur.

An important feature recently highlighted in the literature is that coercion is not a binary phenomenon which either does or does not take place. Rather, it has been argued that coercion is a matter of degree and occurs on a cline (Yoon 2012; Leclercq 2019, 2024a; Busso, Perek and Lenci 2021; and references cited therein). Some of the examples discussed in the context of coercion show such a high degree of incompatibility that it has been questioned whether they are in fact acceptable at all. Consider the following cases.

(24)   ??Farmer Joe *grew* those vines onto his roof. (Goldberg 1995: 169)

(25)   a.   ??Ed hammered the metal *safe*. (Boas 2011: 1271)
       b.   The door of Ed's old Dodge had a piece of metal sticking out. When getting out of the car, Ed had cut himself on the metal and had to go to the hospital to get stitches. The next day, Ed hammered the metal *safe*. (Boas, 2011: 1271)

Goldberg (1995: 169), for instance, argues that the sentence in (24) is hardly acceptable given that the action denoted by the verb *grow* does not readily occur in the semantic frames of causation and directionality activated by the CAUSED-MOTION construction. Likewise, Boas (2011: 1271) acknowledges that the adjective *safe* in (25a) does not appear to be an acceptable candidate for the resultative argument of *hammer*. Yet, context permitting, coercion is not impossible in these cases either. Yoon (2012) provides evidence that the sentence in

---

[9] This use of the construction seems to have become conventional as it is now very frequent to see 'what-about' being used as a verb, especially on social media such as X. This does nothing to diminish the fact that the first uses of this pattern were coined via coercion. That the use of this construction remains unusual here is shown in the use of quotes in the original (though recent) X post.

(24) becomes acceptable when embedded in some specific contexts, such as 'if the situation is that Joe used wires and bars to support the vines so that they can reach the roof' (Yoon, 2012: 5). Boas (2011) makes a similar empirical observation and shows that sentence (25a) becomes perfectly acceptable when properly contextualised, such as in (25b). These examples thus show that some coercive events are more problematic than others, with mismatches that are harder to resolve.

Importantly, coercion is a phenomenon that does not solely involve the narrow (i.e., linguistic) context, but in fact rests upon the broad (i.e., extra-linguistic) context as well. This raises the question of whether coercion is more about breaking the rules or bending the rules. In the recent literature, this question has been addressed through the lens of the notion of *creativity*. Creative cognition is a domain-general process that consists in producing original thoughts, whether it be for problem solving, artistic expression, or other daily activities, through a subtle interplay of novelty and appropriateness (Hoffmann 2020a, in press). Work by Sampson (2016) served as an impetus for a comprehensive approach to linguistic creativity in CxG. Sampson (2016) proposed a distinction between two types of (linguistic) creativity, namely F(ixed)-creativity and E(nlarging/extending)-creativity. F-creativity refers to 'activities which characteristically produce examples drawn from a fixed and known . . . range' while E-creativity refers to 'activities which characteristically produce examples that enlarge our understanding of the range of possible products of the activity' (Sampson 2016: 19). Cases of mismatch and coercion are typically considered cases of F-creativity (Bergs 2019), or in our own words *rule-bending*, given that they produce examples that still fit within the fixed range of possibilities offered by the linguistic system. Bergs (2019: 179–180), however, remarks that not all cases of coercion are F-creative to the same degree, and in fact some instances are difficult to categorise: for instance, he argues that while *laugh yourself off the chair* can be easily described as an F-creative construct, *read yourself off the chair* requires more cognitive effort and comes closer to what would fall under the category of E-creative constructs. Our comparisons of the examples (18–23) and (24–25) align with these remarks, leading us to crucially argue alongside Bergs (2019) that the relationship between F- and E-creativity is not a dichotomy, but a continuum from playing 'by the rules' to playing 'with the rules' (Cappelle 2020; see Bergs and Kompa 2020: 17 for a critical discussion). Importantly, these observations highlight that cases of F-creativity appear to primarily rely on considerations of narrow context, while cases of E-creativity appear to rely on considerations of the broad context to a greater extent. This falls in line with the view that coercion is not a discrete process but that there is a cline of coercion effects.

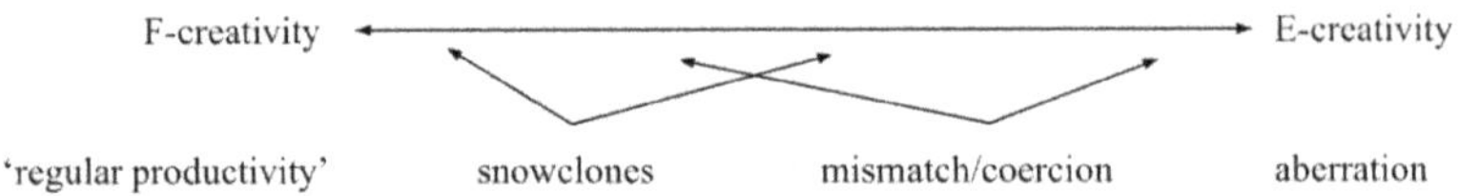

Figure 3 The cline from F- to E-creativity (adapted from Bergs 2019: 181).

Coercion is but one example of functional innovation and creativity. There is an array of other phenomena that can also be analysed as creative uses of language. Bergs (2019: 181) identifies at least three other processes, alongside coercion, which he locates on the cline from F-creative uses to E-creative uses: 'regular productivity', snow clones, and aberration.

As shown on the left side of the cline in Figure 3, traditional conceptions of productivity as linguistic creativity constitute the most fixed type of creative language use. That is because regular productivity simply follows from the existing knowledge speakers have of constructional use. Then, the further we move from the F-pole of the cline, the closer we get to clear deviations from conventional language use. First, distributed along the fixed side of the cline, 'snowclones' stand out as 'schemas that grow from relatively fixed micro-constructions that are usually formulae or clichés' (Traugott and Trousdale 2013: 150). For example, from the construct *He's not the sharpest tool in the shed*, which entails that the subject referent is 'not intelligent', a productive schema is derived (*not the* ADJ*est* N1 *in the* N2) that can be used to express a similar meaning. This is the case for instance for *He's not the quickest bunny in the warren*. As shown in Figure 3, snowclones may be used more or less creatively. Indeed, Bergs (2019: 177) argues, 'there seems to be some sort of gradient between the "regular" and entirely predictable use of snowclones at the one end, and the most unexpected and creative uses, which [tamper] with meaning, form, or both, at the other end'. The *bunny* example just presented represents a case of fairly regular (i.e., F-creative) use of the snowclone. More enlarging (i.e., E-creative) uses of the snowclone include examples such as the following:

(26) He is not the hottest marshmallow in the fire. (Bergs 2019: 177)

(27) Actually, he is the dimmest bulb in the basement. (Hoffmann in press)

The example in (26) shows a use of the snowclone which tampers with its meaning. The speaker does not construe the subject referent as 'not very intelligent' but as 'not (sexually) very attractive'. The example in (27) illustrates form tampering, by using a positive rather than a negative declarative clause. In addition, it may be argued that meaning is also affected, with low intelligence being represented as the lowest value on a scale. Compared to the previous *bunny* example, these two cases come across as more (E-)creative uses of the snowclone.

An interesting feature, not listed by Bergs but identified as a key component in the use of snowclones, is that of 'extravagance' (Hartmann and Ungerer, 2023). Extravagance is a notion inspired by one of Keller's maxims of language known as 'talk in such a way that you are noticed' (Keller 1994; Haspelmath 1999). It is identified as one of three features of snowclones by Hartmann and Ungerer (2023: 28), and is especially prevalent in so-called E-creative snowclones, as is to be expected from the observation that extravagance is associated with E-creativity more generally (Ungerer and Hartmann 2023). In Bergs' taxonomy, the most E-creative uses of language come in the form of what he calls 'aberrations', namely 'uses that apparently do not conform to any (obvious) linguistic rule and that are not subject to any (obvious) constraints' (Bergs 2019: 180). Examples of aberrations include the very first uses of the now well-known X *much?* construction (e.g., *Racist much?*) and sentence-final *not* (e.g., *I really enjoyed the film. Not.*), which were originally not licensed by the linguistic system. They also include experimental forms of poetic language, such as James Joyce's stream of consciousness prose or Hugo Ball's dadaist aesthetics (Bergs 2018; Hoffmann 2020a).

Bergs (2018: 279) also mentions errors and mistakes as another potential source of E-creativity. He argues for instance that so-called 'malaphors' (i.e,. unintentional blended idioms) are good examples of such creative constructs. Consider the following example:

(28) I don't give a rat's crap.[10]

This example contains a blend of the idioms *I don't give a crap* and *I don't give a rat's ass*, both of which express the meaning of 'not caring', the main difference being that the latter sounds less polite than the former. This blend, which potentially results from self-correction (as used by the American pastor Mark Burns), is novel. The question though is to know whether it actually is creative. First of all, it is not functionally innovative. Most importantly, this blend was probably not produced intentionally. Yet, it appears that the 'intentional manipulation of linguistic material' (Bergs 2018: 280) constitutes a central feature of linguistic creativity. Intentionality has been subject to discussions in CxG approaches to creativity, especially regarding whether it is a necessary or a sufficient criterion (Bergs 2018; Hoffmann 2020b; Uhrig 2020). Bergs (2018: 279) considers that examples like (28) might not count as cases of creative use of language, and we agree that malaphors are not typically creative. By comparison,

---

[10] From: https://malaphors.com/2024/03/04/i-dont-give-a-rats-crap/. Last accessed 9 April 2024.

we find that constructs such as *How very dare you!?*, innovated in the comedic *Catherine Tate Show*, are indeed creative. This construct is grammatically unacceptable, as evinced by reactions observed in Hoffmann (2020b: 1), since adverbs (with the exception of *not*) cannot modify an auxiliary in English. This construct is appropriately used by the character Derek Faye however, who uses the adverb *very* as an intensifier to convey excessive indignation. This functional innovation is accepted by the audience thanks to its comical effect, which highlights the creative potential of humour (Brône 2017).

Finally, it is important to note that functional innovations and creativity can occur not only in the specific processes of coercion, snowclones, and aberrations but also in other pervasive processes in common language use. For example, metaphors and metonymies, reviewed in the previous section, can feature varying degrees of novelty.

(29)   Yeah that's really what I was getting at. I almost . . . couldn't pull apart coffee from caffeine, because I'm a *muggle* in this subject matter.[11]

(30)   Don't look now, but Bulging Biceps is smiling at you.[12]

In (29), an excerpt from the popular podcast *Diary of a CEO*, the host draws a metaphorical mapping between 'muggles' (a term used in the Harry Potter universe to refer to individuals who do not possess magical abilities) and 'outsiders' (in this case, someone who is not an expert on the topic of coffee) to highlight his unfamiliarity with the distinction between coffee and caffeine. The metaphorical mapping between 'wizards' and 'skill/ability' is not uncommon, as shown by the use of the construction 'N *wizard*' such as in *computer wizard, guitar wizard*, or *Wall Street wizard*. However, what is less common is the metaphorical mapping between 'wizard' and 'expertise', and in particular between 'non-wizard' and 'lack of expertise', which constitutes the innovative meaning feature of *muggle* here. By contrast, the example in (30) contains what we may consider an innovative metonymy, although this needs to be explained further. Indeed, the metonymy draws on the established 'BODY PART for PERSON' mapping, and as such does not establish a completely new metonymic relationship. According to Brdar (2018), new metonymies are hardly ever possible to innovate, which we note as an important difference from metaphors. Littlemore (2022) concurs that new conceptual metonymies are nearly impossible to find, but she points out that speakers can use them creatively by extending them to new lexical items. In the case of (30), the body part *biceps* is not a typical lexical

---

[11]   From the podcast *The Diary of A CEO* (episode "The Coffee Expert: The Surprising Link Between Coffee & Your Mental Health! James Hoffmann", https://youtu.be/TqNrJNhcf5g?si=_l6sChjh_5bKPbKn&t=1167). Last accessed 23 January 2024.
[12]   From https://dailytrope.com/category/metonymy, Last accessed 25 March 2024.

instantiation of the 'BODY PART for PERSON' conceptual metonymy, and this instantiation thus appears to have been innovated by the speaker. It is all the more creative that the body part 'biceps' is here qualified by a descriptive adjective (*bulging*) and that the whole noun phrase is in fact used as a proper noun.

3.3 Meaning Change

So far we have focused on meaning in use from a synchronic perspective, and a crucial insight is that meaning 'varies' as it is constructed in context. Here, we want to expand on the idea that meaning drives grammar (Section 2.1), by considering that meaning variation is often a precursor for lexical and grammatical change. Before discussing these processes, it is important to consider that meaning itself is subject to change.

Meaning change can be observed across the constructicon, from the more lexical to the more grammatical constructions. One of the simplest examples of meaning change in the former type includes words that have not changed in form but have developed distinct, diachronically related meanings. Let us discuss the lexemes *virus*, *call*, and *cool* as cases in point. The noun *virus* can refer to an 'extremely small piece of organic material that causes disease in humans, animals, and plants' or 'a computer program or part of a computer program that can make copies of itself and is intended to prevent the computer from working normally', among others.[13] The second meaning historically emerged from the first, and appears to have been established through a metaphorical mapping between the frames of biological organisms and computer programmes. Likewise, the verb *call* may have developed one of its modern meanings ('to use a phone to talk to someone') as a metaphorical extension (in the telecommunication frame) of one of its earlier meanings, namely that of 'know[ing] or address[ing] someone by a particular name'.[14] Notably, this latter meaning has itself evolved and now also refers to cases where a device other than a phone is used for multimodal communication (e.g., with a computer via Skype, Zoom, or Teams). Finally, the adjective *cool* has undergone a more complex series of meaning changes (Moore 2004; Tagliamonte and Pabst 2020). This adjective was initially used to describe a slightly cold temperature and came to be used metaphorically to refer to someone's 'emotional control, detachment, knowingness and deviance from the mainstream', especially among African American speakers in the US from

---

[13] From https://dictionary.cambridge.org/dictionary/english/virus. Last accessed 9 April 2024.
[14] From https://dictionary.cambridge.org/dictionary/english/call. Last accessed 9 April 2024.

the 1930s onwards (Moore 2004: 79). The positive tone of this variant in turn gave rise to *cool* as a general adjective of high positive evaluation.

The examples in the previous paragraph concern meaning changes occurring for established lexical units. There are cases in which change in meaning occurs in tandem with change in form, and there are three notable types of such cases that we want to focus on here. The first type is typically discussed in terms of lexical constructionalisation (Traugott and Trousdale 2013: 192). This process is best illustrated in the emergence of the noun *cupboard*. As Traugott and Trousdale (2013: 22) show, *cupboard* originated from the combination of the two independent words *cup* (/ˈkʌp/) and *board* (/ˈbɔːd/) into the endocentric compound *cupboard*, which referred to a piece of wood on which cups are displayed. It then went through a semantic shift and its meaning became non-compositional (in referring to any closed storage area not exclusive to cups) as well as a formal shift from compound to simplex word (which involves a phonological reduction in /ˈkʌbəd/). Another more recent example is the verb *gaslight*. Before the creation of electric lighting, incandescent gas lamps were used for public and private lighting, hence the nouns *gas lighting* and *gas light*. This term featured in 1939 as the title of a play by Patrick Hamilton (*Gas Light*), in which a husband manipulates his wife by telling her that the upstairs noises and the apparent dimming of the light are figments of her imagination (when they are in fact his own doing). Similar scenes are included in the 1944 film adaptation *Gaslight*, which then gave rise to the metonymic gerund expression *gaslighting* to refer to 'trick[ing] or control-[ling] someone by making them believe that their memories or beliefs about something are wrong, especially by suggesting that they may be mentally ill'.[15] At that point, the meaning of the construction had shifted by losing its direct reference to the gas lights featured in the play and film. Then over time, especially from the mid-2010s, the verb *to gaslight* was further bleached to include a number of 'loose uses', such as manipulation, emotional abuse, and lying. In this case, meaning change is accompanied by a formal shift from a compositional nominal compound to a non-compositional (simplex) verb. A final example of lexicalisation we want to discuss is the adjective *laughable*. A compositional interpretation of this adjective would involve the addition of the verb *laugh* and the morphological schema V-*able* into the complex meaning 'can be laughed at'. Yet the adjective is not only used to convey this meaning, but contains in addition a feature of ridicule or derision (Hilpert

---

[15] From https://dictionary.cambridge.org/fr/dictionnaire/anglais/gaslight. Last accessed 16 April 2024.

2019: 99). This leads to storing *laughable* as a distinct lexical item separately from the individual constituting parts.[16]

Further up the constructicon, the second type of meaning/form changes concerns cases of lexico-grammatical constructionalisation. Here, we will especially be interested in the emergence of new morphological schemas. Traugott and Trousdale (2013: 170) for instance discuss the development of the schema N-*dom* as a case in point. They explain that in Old English, the noun *dom* was used as a free lexeme to express a range of meanings such as 'doom, judgment, authority to judge' (170), as illustrated in example (31). It then started to be used as the right element of a compound, such as in example (32).

(31) for   ðam   ðe   hit   is   Godes   ***dom***
      for   that   that   it   is   God.GEN   law.NOM
      'Because it is God's law' (Deut (c1000 OE Heptateuch) B 8. 1.4.5 [DOEC])

(32) a. for   ðan   þe   he   æfter   cristes   þrowunge   ærest
         for   that   that he after   Christ.GEN   suffering   first
         martyr|dom   geðrowade
         martyr|dom   suffered
         'because he was the first to suffer martyrdom after Christ's suffering' (c1000
         ÆCHom I.3 [DOEC])
     b. Ðæt   is   se   ***freodom***   ðætte mon   mot   don   ðæt
         that   is   the   freedom.NOM   that   man.NOM may.3S   do.INF   that
         he   wile.
         he   want.3SPres
         'That is freedom, that a man may do as he will'. (c890 Boethius B.9.3.2
         [DOEC])

The two examples in (32) show that -*dom* could be used in compounds with both nouns (e.g., *martyr*) and adjectives (e.g., *freo* 'free'), which became a starting point for the process of constructionalisation of -*dom* into an 'affixoid' (Booij 2010). The use of -*dom* with adjectives was soon restricted to a small number of highly frequent types which then lexicalised (such as *freedom* and *wisdom*). It is with nominals that -*dom* started to gain in productivity in Old English, especially with the meanings 'state' and 'condition', and then came to express 'jurisdiction of a N, territory of a N' in

---

[16] There are other types of lexical constructionalisation which involve the instantaneous addition of a completely new form–meaning pair in the constructicon. These include for instance borrowings from another language (e.g., *sushi, table, devour*), acronyms (*wags, scuba*), or invented words (e.g., brand names such as *Xerox*) (Traugott and Trousdale 2013: 29–30). Similarly, degrammaticalisation phenomena (e.g., the evolution of *ish*, Norde 2009: 223) appear to be best understood as specific instances of lexical constructionalisation (Traugott and Trousdale 2013: 190). These fall beyond the scope of this section.

Middle English. The suffix is still productive in Present Day English, but started to be associated with a pejorative evaluation alongside the more general meaning 'realm of' (Marchand 1969: 263; Trips 2009) such as in *bumbledom* or *gangsterdom* (Traugott and Trousdale 2013: 176). More recent examples include *Blairdom* or *Obamadom* (Traugott and Trousdale 2013: 68). An example from the NOW corpus contains the following instance:

(33)   From her cheap red MAGA baseball cap – and no, it isn't 'elitist' to pine for the days when elected leaders dressed like adults inside the Capitol – to her many loud buttons, to her T-shirt adorned with a slogan plucked directly from **wokedom** circa 2020, 'Say Her Name,' in reference to Laken Riley, Greene put on a clinic of unsightliness. (NOW)

The emergence of the morphological schema X-*gate* constitutes a more recent case of lexico-grammatical constructionalisation. This construction is known to have originated from the Watergate scandal in the US in 1972–1974, involving President Nixon. In the following years, the noun *Watergate* was reanalysed into a schema (X-*gate*) whose meaning shifted to 'a scandal involving X' (Joseph 1998: 360). This reanalysis took place as the schema was increasingly used in (analogical) coinages such as *Koreagate* (1976), *Billygate* (1980), *Irangate* (1980), and *sewergate* (1983) (Joseph 1992: 222). Though initial uses of the schema contained proper nouns, it extended to common nouns as well, as shown in the last example. Nowadays, it remains a productive schema, and recent examples include *donutgate* (in 2015, involving the singer Ariana Grande), *Melaniagate* (in 2016, involving the first lady of the USA Melania Trump), *bagelgate* (in 2019, involving ways of slicing bagels in the US), and *Partygate* (in 2021, involving the UK prime minister Boris Johnson). This is why Ungerer and Hartmann (2023: 45) argue that new formations 'are not coined in analogy to *Watergate* anymore but rather make use of a schema [X-*gate*] that is now independent from its source'.

The last example of lexico-grammatical contructionalisation we want to discuss is the morphological schema *cyber*-N. This schema stems from the truncated use of the noun *cybernetics*, a term coined in the late 1940s to refer to the nascent field of control and communication theory in computer science. Although the term harks back to the Ancient Greek noun *kubernētikos* ('the art of steering'), its meaning is not compositional. However, English speakers came to reanalyse *cybernetics* as including the prefix *cyber*-, associating it predominantly with the meaning 'virtual/online'. Over the course of the second half of the twentieth century, the prefix *cyber*-X became a very productive morphological template, licensing coinages such as *cyberspace, cyberattack, cyberbullying, cyberactivities, cybercampaign,* and *cyberfriendship.*

The examples considered in the lexico-grammatical category constitute cases of increased schematicity, although the constructions retain a primarily lexical meaning. However, schematicity is typically a property of grammatical constructions, and schematisation generally features as part of the development of grammatical meaning (see, for example, Croft 2001: 16; Langacker 2008: 22; Traugott 2008: 34, 2015: 61; Trousdale 2008a: 59, 2008b: 304, 2010: 51, 2012: 168; Coussé, Andersson and Olofsson 2018a; Leclercq 2024a: 150).[17] This has been discussed in the context of grammatical constructionalisation, which is the third type of meaning change considered in this section. While many things could be said about the cognitive mechanisms involved and the formal changes at play in the process of grammatical constructionalisation (see Gildea and Barðdal 2023 and references cited therein), here we focus on the dimension of meaning.

Grammatical constructionalisation takes place when a lexical construction comes to be used with a grammatical function. This raises the question of what counts as grammatical meaning.[18] In the literature, grammatical meaning is sometimes defined as being more abstract or schematic than lexical meaning – a view which is also found in cognitive linguistics in general and CxG in particular (Langacker 2008: 178, Trousdale 2008b: 317). Schematicity or abstractness of meaning does not suffice to distinguish between grammatical and lexical meaning, however (Boye and Harder 2012; Leclercq 2024a: 157). Instead, we prefer Bybee's (2006b) more comprehensive formulation, which states that 'grammatical meaning is more abstract, more generalised, more subjective and discourse-oriented than lexical meaning' (187). Besides increased abstractness, this formulation aptly highlights the associated processes of subjectification and pragmatic strengthening, which have been identified as central to grammaticalisation (Diewald 2011). The first of these two processes, subjectification, has been addressed in two distinct ways in the literature. According to Langacker (1990, 2011), grammatical constructions are more subjective in the sense that they do not constitute the explicit object of conceptualization but only 'serve to abet and supplement [the description of lexical items]' (Langacker 2011: 82). By contrast, in Traugott's (1995, 2010) approach, grammatical constructions tend to be more subjective by virtue of indexing the speaker's attitudes and beliefs. The second of these processes,

---

[17] Though see Noël (2007) for a critical discussion.

[18] Grammatical meaning is sometimes equated with *procedural* meaning in CxG (e.g., Traugott and Trousdale 2013; Coussé, Andersson and Oloffson 2018b). We discuss this terminological alternative in the concluding chapter.

pragmatic strengthening, relates to the particular way in which specific implicatures become part of the meaning of a construction. We now discuss two specific examples to illustrate these processes in the context of grammatical constructionalisation.

An often discussed case of grammatical constructionalisation is the development of the future construction BE *going to* (see Traugott 2015 and Budts and Petré 2016 for recent overviews). This construction initially emerged from the use of the motion-encoding lexical verb *go* in purposive contexts (e.g., *I am going to London to marry Bill*; Hopper and Traugott 2003: 3). These contexts paved the way for a grammaticalisation process: indeed, purposives invite an inference of futurity that gradually came to be part of the meaning of the construction BE *going to* (a case of pragmatic strengthening), alongside which the verb simultaneously lost its specific meaning of 'motion' (a case of semantic bleaching). Specifically, the futurity meaning of this new construction includes the notion of future intentions, which is directly inherited as a constraint from the original purposive use (Hopper and Traugott 2003: 3). This is illustrated in Bybee (2006a: 720) with example (34):

(34) *Duke*   Sir Valentine, whither away so fast?
      Val.   Please it your grace, there is a messenger
                That stays in to bear my letters to my friends,
                And I **am going to** deliver them.
                                 (1595, Shakespeare, Two gentlemen of Verona, III.i.51)

While the Duke enquires where Valentine is going, Valentine's answer 'does not specify location, but rather intention' (Bybee 2006a: 720). The use of BE *going to* to express future intentions can be viewed as an instance of subjectification in the Langackerian sense, with the loss of reference to an independent event (i.e., spatial 'go') in favour of a certain bracketing of another event (e.g., 'deliver', as in (34)). In later stages, the construction also went through a process of subjectification as defined by Traugott, in the sense that the future meaning became increasingly couched in the speaker's beliefs towards the proposition (Budts and Petré 2016: 21–22). For indeed, because the construction was increasingly used to discuss other people's intentions, an epistemic value was added that indexed the speaker's uncertainty towards the subject's intentions. The growth of this epistemic value and the weakening of the intentional reading then caused 'invited inferences of prediction and future to develop' (Budts and Petré 2016: 22), and BE *going to* gradually came to be used as a future expression of evidence-based prediction. The emergence of this grammatical meaning is part of a process of grammatical constructionalisation in which the formal dimension is also affected. Besides the neo-analysis of BE *going to* as one symbolic unit, the construction underwent auxiliarisation (Krug 2000). On the one hand, this involves schematisation via host-class expansion such that language users know the partially schematic construction BE *going to* V-INF (see Hilpert 2016 and Leclercq 2023b for similar analyses of modal verb constructions), and on the other hand, further changes involve univerbation and reduction (e.g., the phonologically coalesced form *gonna*).[19]

As a second example, let us consider aspects of the meaning of the construction *a lot of* as it evolved from a binominal partitive to a quantifier conveying a large quantity (Brems 2011, 2012; Traugott and Trousdale 2013; Cuyckens 2018). Initially, *hlot* in Old English was a fully lexical construction which referred to 'an object, often a piece of wood, by which individuals were selected, e.g., for office, often with appeals to God (cf. *draw lots, lottery, lot* 'fate')' (Traugott and Trousdale 2013: 23). This meaning was extended by metonymy to refer to the unit acquired in this manner (e.g., *a lot of land* referring to a piece of land owned by the recipient), which then favoured the emergence of partitive interpretations. An initial partitive reading involved the basic identification of a part within a larger whole, such as in example (35) discussed by Brems (2012: 217). A subsequent interpretation identified a more specific partitive relation by explicitly viewing the part as referring to 'a unit consisting of several members' (Cuyckens 2018: 187), such as in example (36) discussed by Traugott and Trousdale (2013: 24).

(35) For to forwerrpenn **anig lott Off Moysœsess lare**
      'For to reject any part of Moses' teaching'
      (PPCME, *The Ormulum*, c1200)

(36) You must tell Edward that my father gives 25s. a piece to Seward for his last ***lot of***
      sheep, and, in return for this news, my father wishes to receive some of Edward's
      pigs. (1798 Austen, Letter to her sister [CL])

It is from the latter use that a notion of particularly large quantities was inferred and that the use of *a lot of* as a quantifier started to emerge. The example in (37) highlights the salience of the 'large quantity' implicature. This eventually constituted the primary meaning of a new quantifying construction, illustrated in (38), for which *many* and *much* are considered typical substitutes (Brems 2012: 218, Traugott and Trousdale 2013: 25).

---

[19] One question that has received increasing attention in the literature is whether contracted variants (e.g., *gonna*) of modal verbs (e.g., *be going to*) are simply more auxiliarised realisations or whether they display meaning differences that justify their being considered constructions of their own (Lorenz 2013, Levshina and Lorenz 2022, Daugs 2023, Mikkelsen and Morin in press).

(37) I bought **a lot of clothes** of the shopman, and took them to the stable (OBC, 1820s). (Brems 2012: 217)

(38) He is only young, with ***a lot of power*** (1895 Meredith, The Amazing Marriage (CL 3)). (Traugott and Trousdale 2013: 25)

Similarly to BE *going to*, the grammaticalisation of the *a lot of* construction reflects the central processes of meaning change introduced in the foregoing paragraphs. It involves both semantic bleaching (in the loss of referential content) and pragmatic strengthening (in the conventionalisation of an implicature). In addition, processes of subjectification are at play. There is subjectification in the Langackerian sense, since the object of conceptualisation is now offstage and must be specified by a distinct lexical item (e.g., *power* in (38)). It also involves a process of subjectification as understood by Traugott, in that *a lot of* does not have a referential value but indexes the speaker's assessment of a quantity of things. Here again, the meaning changes are closely intertwined with changes in form. Cuyckens (2018: 191) lists three notable changes: increased schematicity, increased productivity, and decreased compositionality. The construction has indeed gained in formal schematicity since the grammaticalised unit now requires that a nominal head be selected (i.e., speakers actually know the partially schematic form '*a lot of* N'). It has also gained in productivity, as the types of nouns that can occur with the quantifier has increased to include not only concrete nouns but also abstract nouns. Finally, it has lost in compositionality, both from the perspective of form and meaning, as it no longer features the binominal head–modifier structure [*a lot* [*of* NP]], and thus its meaning cannot be predicted from its component parts anymore. Overall, this loss of compositionality is also evidenced by the occasional realisation of *a lot of* as the coalesced and reduced variant *lotta/alotta*, which appears to be specific to rapid and informal speech (Traugott and Trousdale 2013: 211; Cuyckens 2018: 186).

So far, the examples of grammatical constructionalisation that we have described show the evolution from a lexical item to a grammatical construction. It has long been acknowledged however that grammaticalisation may also involve a change 'from a less grammatical to a more grammatical status' (Kuryłowicz 1965: 69). In the literature, the first type of grammaticalisation (from lexical to grammatical) is sometimes labelled 'primary' grammaticalisation, while the second type (from 'less' grammatical to 'more' grammatical) is called 'secondary' grammaticalisation (Givón 1991: 305, Traugott 2002: 25–27). Whether a strict distinction between these two processes should be maintained remains a matter of debate (see for example Breban 2014 and Smirnova 2015 for discussion). The point remains that some grammatical constructions emerge from lexical sources while others grow out of already grammaticalised constructions. It is instances of this latter process, 'secondary' grammaticalisation, that we would like to dwell on before concluding this section.

Given that secondary grammaticalisation consists in a shift from one grammatical construction to another, one may wonder whether a formal change is involved in this process or whether only meaning is affected. Although there exist different approaches in the literature, they converge in identifying changes that occur on both levels. At the formal level, this process is traditionally assumed to increase morphophonological and morphosyntactic bondedness towards cliticisation and inflectionalisation (Norde 2012). This view can be found in early work by Traugott (2002), who initially adhered to the hypothesis of unidirectionality (from lexical sources to bonded grammatical elements). As she increasingly couched her findings in a constructional perspective, Traugott's (2024) view departed from this hypothesis though. The constructional view of secondary grammaticalisation is best illustrated, we find, in later work by Smirnova (2015), who shows that this process is more aptly described as involving both constructionalisation and constructional changes. In this view, secondary grammaticalization takes a grammatical source construction and returns another grammatical construction, which need not be bonded. Likewise, at the meaning level, secondary grammaticalisation appears to correlate with similar types of meaning change as primary grammaticalisation, namely semantic bleaching and pragmatic strengthening (Smirnova 2015: 222). By means of illustration, concessive constructions with *may* and *might* will now be considered.

Modal auxiliary verbs in English are considered to be the 'paradigm case of grammaticization' (Plank 1984: 308). Specifically here, they are a paradigm case of primary grammaticalisation. Recently, Leclercq (2024b) claims that *may* and *might* are currently going through a process of secondary grammaticalisation, in examples like (39) and (40).

(39) I don't like this. Those guys may be helping us, but they're breaking the law. (TV, 1994)

(40) The only thing I had liked about this case was the octopus. She might be crooked and a killer, but how could one judge a creature like her? (FIC, 2017)

Leclercq (2024b: 153) argues that in such factual concessives, *may* and *might* are not used as epistemic markers to judge the likelihood of the proposition to be true, but they serve as polite discursive markers to hedge the contrast between the conceded proposition and the asserted one. In doing so, he demonstrates that not only is there semantic bleaching since the concept of possibility typically associated with the two verbs is pushed out, but there is also pragmatic strengthening through a change in scope from the propositional domain to the discursive domain with an increase in intersubjectivity (150). The latter process is of particular importance as it has been argued that (increased) intersubjectivity, namely 'the explicit expression of the [speaker's] attention to the 'self' of [the addressee]' (Traugott 2003: 128), is a distinct functional trait of secondary grammaticalisation (e.g., Narrog 2012, 2015, 2017).[20] At the formal level, secondary grammaticalisation is assumed to come with processes of constructionalisation and constructional changes (Smirnova 2015). Leclercq (2024b: 151) argues that this is the case here, with the initial development of the distinct hedged concessive constructions 'SUBJ *may* VP, *but*-CLAUSE' and 'SUBJ *might* VP, *but*-CLAUSE', and the latter expansion (and schematisation) to clauses introduced by any of the typical concessive markers (e.g., *while, although, though, despite*, and so forth), as in examples (41) and (42):

(41) We knew Jon would come back different and **while** his transformation *may* not be as extreme as some had predicted, this is definitely a darker Lord Commander. (MAG, 2016)

(42) And though I may complain, **though** I *may* envy her face, I love Ella as if she were my own child. (FIC, 1994)

3.4 Summary

In this section, we described some of the central mechanisms that structure meaning in language use as viewed by CxG. We paid particular attention to three domains. First, we stressed that meaning is constructed in context by both the hearer and the speaker. It is enabled by distinct cognitive processes, and it features certain constraints that delimit the generative potential of the constructional network. Second, these constraints notwithstanding, we highlighted the innovative potential of making meaning as a creative activity of language users, who can bend or break the rules of constructional use for different communicative and social purposes. Thirdly and finally, we fully shifted our focus from the individual to the community. We showed that the malleable nature of meaning also leads to specific processes of change over time that contribute to (re) shaping the linguistic system.

---

[20] There is as of yet no full consensus on the status of intersubjectivity in secondary grammaticalisation though, and it has been argued that other types of meaning change such as 'objectification' might be at play (see Kranich 2008, 2010; Breban 2014: 484–487). Interestingly, Traugott (2010: 34) observes that Nuyts' (2005: 18) definition of intersubjectivity 'intersects with objectivity'. So these two views seem compatible.

Section 2 identified the central role of the meaning-based assumption in CxG. The current section completed this picture by shedding light on the dynamic nature of meaning as being (co-)constructed in context. This is where our literature review ends, and we step in with what we believe are the limitations of the current framework. In Section 4, we address several salient points of contention and inconsistencies regarding views of meaning in the constructional approach, and we make suggestions for a fine-tuned model of meaning in CxG.

4 A Framework of Constructional Meaning

4.1 Types of Meaning: Drawing a Line

The first three sections of this Element presented a broadly consensual overview of what constitutes meaning from a CxG perspective. Section 4 will focus on aspects of meaning that are either points of disagreement, grey areas, or more recent developments. Our attention will first be given to the way that meaning is modelled.

In traditional approaches to linguistics, a basic introductory assumption in the study of meaning is the distinction between semantics and pragmatics. This assumption has taken two main shapes: one can either view the distinction between semantics and pragmatics as a distinction between conventional and inferred contextual meaning, or one can view this distinction as one between truth-conditional and non-truth-conditional meaning (Huang 2014: 299). These two views, though relying on crucially different criteria, have been shown to be complementary (see, for example, Finkbeiner 2019 and Leclercq 2020 for recent discussions from a constructionist perspective). Notwithstanding, the idea prevails in CxG that a strict semantics/pragmatics distinction should be rejected (Goldberg 1995: 7; Langacker 2008: 40; Auf der Straße 2017: 61; Ariel 2023: 275). This is precisely why so far we have refrained from using the terms 'semantic' and 'pragmatic' when discussing constructional meaning. Yet exactly what this theoretical stance entails needs to be addressed as it is not without its problems.

One of the important questions that is raised is whether the two views presented in the previous paragraph are equally rejected, and if not, to what extent each might be. The first view, operationalised in terms of conventionality, is rejected for at least two reasons. One is that conventionality is not a categorical feature. Some aspects of meaning are more or less conventional or contextual (Langacker 2008: 40). In the recent CxG literature (Hilpert 2018, 2021; Hilpert and Flach 2023; Ungerer 2023), it has actually been argued that constructions should not be conceived as categorical signs that either associate a form and a meaning or don't (a node-centred view) but preferably as forms that are linked more or less strongly to specific meanings (a link-centred view).[21] The other is that conventionality and context-dependence are not separate features, but meaning conventions are integrated in a context-sensitive process of meaning construction (see Section 3.1). In that sense, CxG 'is therefore most radically contextualist' (Leclercq 2024c), given that meaning conventions are not purely linguistic, context-free objects but they are inherently context-sensitive.[22] What this shows is that the first view is not, in effect, completely dismissed but just qualified so as to be less stringent. A gradient approach is thus preferred to the strict distinction between conventionality and context dependence. In keeping with Leclercq (2020: 229), we believe there is a potential limit to this approach though. It is indeed one thing to posit a gradient from conventional to context-dependent features of meaning. However, if one's interest lies in the study of constructions, in the technical sense of the term (cf. Section 1), then one is by definition compelled to identify *conventional* features of meaning. So in spite of its being a gradient, the semantics/pragmatics distinction as defined in terms of conventionality thus cannot entirely be discarded and remains relevant, and we concur with Ungerer (2023) that even in a gradient approach, the idea of a threshold remains important for identifying what counts as a construction or not. So the first view cannot and should not be rejected.

The second view, operationalised in terms of truth conditionality, is more explicitly rejected by the constructionist approach. As mentioned in Section 2.3, it is generally considered that meaning is not defined by truth conditions but rather by construals (Goldberg 2013: 16). In contrast with view 1, distinguishing between truth-conditional (semantic) and non-truth-conditional (pragmatic) meaning is therefore considered entirely misguided. This assumption still appears to be foundational today, as shown in Boas, Leino and Lyngfelt (2024: 6), who point out that it remains questionable whether 'CxG should distinguish between "semantic" and "pragmatic" types of meaning'. However, as Gonzálvez-García (2020: 112) has pointed out,

> the treatment of semantic and/or pragmatic facts in [cognitive construction grammar] is at best somewhat inconsistent with the theoretical premises invoked. As Cappelle (2017, 144) has rightly put it: 'on the one hand,

---

[21] Hilpert (2021: 72) dubs this the 'fat node problem'. Beyond the issue at stake here, this problem concerns all types of links that a particular form can establish (cf. Hilpert and Flach 2023). These other applications of the gradient, link-centred view are beyond the scope of our discussion.

[22] Interestingly, note that the constructional approach is also radically contextualist at the formal level, given that conventions regarding the form of a construction are not solely linguistic but also include any other relevant cue from context such as intonation, gaze, co-speech gesture, etc. This multimodal approach, though more recent in the theory (cf. Hoffmann 2021), appears to follow naturally from its usage-based premises.

> Goldberg [1995, 7] says that a strict semantics/pragmatics distinction is eschewed but on the other, the list of pragmatic kinds of information is treated as complementing semantic information rather than merging with it to form an undifferentiated bag of functional aspects'.

This is the case for instance in the way that Kay and Michaelis (2012) and Hilpert (2019) respectively analyse the Metalinguistic Negation and the Topicalization constructions.

(43) a. Her name isn't [æn'drijə]; it's [andrej'ə]. (Kay and Michaelis 2012: 2286)
     b. It's not the unique criteria, it's the unique criterion.
     c. The cow isn't pissing, son, she's urinating.

(44) Most heavy metal I don't really like. (Hilpert 2019: 110)

In keeping with Horn (1985), Kay and Michaelis (2012) argue that in (43) the adverb *not* is not used to negate the content of the proposition in the first clause but is instead used to object to extra-propositional features. This includes pronunciation (43a), grammaticality (43b), and register (43c). Regarding example (44), Hilpert (2019) argues that the object constituent used in initial position is topicalised.[23] Such features of information structure are considered inherently pragmatic in CxG (Goldberg 2004, Leino 2013, Hilpert 2019, Hoffmann 2022). Overall, these two examples illustrate that, despite the principled rejection of a truth-conditionally-based distinction between semantic and pragmatic meaning, the way that certain features are explicitly identified as being non-propositional/pragmatic inevitably hinges on truth conditions as a distinguishing factor. Because this distinction appears to be useful, we think it should be modelled more explicitly. Leino (2013: 329) points out that 'information structure is without any doubt the pragmatically oriented phenomenon or subject area that has received the most attention in the context of Construction Grammar'. This is made apparent in introductions to CxG such as Hilpert (2019: 102), which primarily focuses on information packaging when addressing the 'pragmatic side of Construction Grammar'. Perhaps as a result of this relatively limited incorporation of pragmatic meaning, Wen (2022) argues that a full-fledged 'construction pragmatics' needs to be developed. Though we concur with Wen (2022), we also agree with Foolen (2023: 21) that 'there is already more literature available than might be thought at first sight', as shown by recent advances in constructionist models of the semantic/pragmatic interface (e.g., Kay 2004, Nikiforidou 2009, Lee-Goldman 2011, Cappelle and Depraetere 2016, Cappelle 2017, Cappelle, Depraetere and Lesuisse 2019,

---

[23] See also Hoffmann (2022: 228–229) for a similar analysis.

Finkbeiner 2019, Kuzai 2020, Leclercq 2020, 2024a, 2024c, Leclercq, Morin and Pijpops unpublished[24]).

Having shown that both views are viable, two further questions emerge. Firstly, from a terminological and practical standpoint, which of the two views should we implement in future descriptions? The terms *semantics* and *pragmatics* are indeed ambiguous and this ambiguity could negatively affect the theory. Leclercq (2020: 231) argues that

> defining semantics and pragmatics via the lens of conventionality would be rather uninformative in a theory like CxG. Constructions *are* linguistic conventions. ... Instead, constructionists show an increasing need to distinguish between different types of encoded content, and this difference is not accounted for by any other terms in the theory. It seems more appropriate to use the terms *semantics* and *pragmatics* in relation to this difference, which, as mentioned before, relates to truth-conditionality.

This particular stance may be unpopular for card-carrying constructionists because it leads to the second, more critical question: how is this view compatible with the seemingly opposite assumption that the richness of conceptualisations eludes truth conditions? Following Cappelle (2017) and Leclercq (2020), we see no necessary contradiction. In our view, it is possible to maintain that truth conditions do not exhaust the meaning of constructions while arguing that there is a level at which they still play a role. Unlike in traditional truth-conditional semantics, we do not see the language–world relation as more basic than the language–mind relation (see Section 2.3). Quite the contrary, we maintain that the language–mind relation is basic and we fully embrace the view presented in the previous sections. That being said, this by no means entails that the language–world relation is evacuated. Reviewing some of the core tenets of cognitive semantics, Gärdenfors (1999: 21) points out that 'the truth of expressions is considered to be secondary, since truth concerns the relation between the mental structure and the world. To put it tersely: Meaning comes before truth.' We think it is important to uphold this position: the link between language and the world (i.e., truth conditions) persists; it is only not considered as basic. By reversing the precedence relationship between world and mind, there appears to be no theoretical aporia. At the same time, it enables us to redeem what we find to be an important feature of meaning. In our view, truth conditions do contribute to the meaning of constructions, only they show the following characteristics: (i) they are not fully 'objective' (i.e., not fully external to the mind), but reflect cognitive representations; (ii) they are fuzzy,

---

[24] Leclercq, B., Morin, C. & Pijpops, D. Unpublished article entitled 'The principle of no equivalence: an agent-based model'.

much like concepts are (Zadeh 1965, Lakoff 1973); (iii) they are fully contextual, in the sense that they are not fixed but (co-)constructed in context (see Section 3.1). As argued in Leclercq (2020: 232), this approach is compatible both with the theoretical premises of CxG and with recent developments in pragmatic theories.

While doubts have been expressed as to their usefulness, the features of conventionality and truth conditionality appear to be useful even in a theory like CxG. We have argued that the latter feature should be referred to when using the labels 'semantics' and 'pragmatics'. Specifically, it is the notion of semantics that captures truth-conditional meaning. The question now is what are the elements which fall in the category of 'non-truth-conditional'? In general, the label 'pragmatic' has been used as an umbrella term to refer to any non-truth-conditional aspects of meaning. Instead, we believe that a more explicit classification of non-truth-conditional features is needed in order to more clearly establish distinguishing aspects of the meaning of constructions. In our view, in the non-truth-conditional domain, a distinction between pragmatic and social types of meaning needs to be made. We will unpack our view in the following paragraphs, but for the sake of exposition, Figure 4 provides a summary of the types of meaning that we assume a construction can convey.

First, it is important to note that this figure is meant to capture all types of conventional meanings that can be conveyed by a construction. In this view, there are three main types of meaning that a construction can convey: semantic, pragmatic, and social meaning.[25] The upper part of this figure identifies the

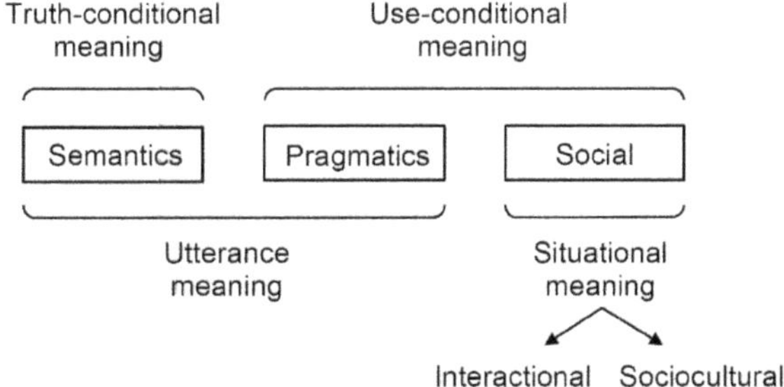

Figure 4 Types of constructional meaning (from Leclercq and Morin 2024).

---

[25] Note that our focus in this Element is on the meaning of constructions, in other words *conventional* meaning rather than non-conventional/inferential meaning. The categories that we present in this section are not limited to the conventional domain, however: the threefold distinction also applies to the inferential domain. We therefore assume that language users can communicate both conventional and inferential semantic, pragmatic, and social meanings.

main distinction introduced earlier through the lens of truth conditionality. Semantic meaning is equated with truth-conditional meaning, while pragmatic meaning and social meaning fall within the domain of non-truth-conditional meaning. In Figure 4, the label 'use-conditional meaning' is introduced in place of the apophatic term 'non-truth-conditional'. This label we borrow from Gutzmann (2015), who himself borrowed it from Recanati (2004) when discussing conventional, non-truth-conditional features of language. Specifically, Gutzmann (2015: 7) defines use-conditional meaning as 'conditions on the felicitous use of the sentence'.[26] Having established this distinction, we believe another conceptual difference enables us to tease apart pragmatic and social meaning. In the lower part of Figure 4, we show that some use conditions still contribute directly to the interpretation of the utterance ('utterance meaning'). These conditions we label as 'pragmatic' meaning features. Pragmatic meaning includes aspects of utterance-focused features such as presupposition, implicatures, illocutionary acts, speaker attitudes, and information structure. In other words, it comprises features that have been traditionally analysed as prototypically pragmatic. We believe that not all use-conditional meanings contribute directly to the interpretation of the utterance however. As shown in the lower part of the figure, there are use-conditional aspects of meaning that rather contribute to interpreting the communicative situation in which the utterance is produced. This corresponds to the category of social meaning (Leclercq and Morin 2023; Leclercq, Morin and Pijpops unpublished). Social meaning, a notion inspired by third-wave variationist sociolinguistic theory (Morin 2023), includes 'inferences about the sort of person who produces the utterance, the situation they are in, the nature of the relationship between interlocutors, the speaker's orientation to the content of the talk, and more' (Hall-lew et al. 2021: 3). In addition, following remarks by Culpeper (2021) on the need to delineate a fine-grained continuum of social context in language use, our model of social meaning is further subdivided into two specific feature types. The first one, 'interactional' social meaning, includes features such as register, genre, style, and activity type (Levinson 1992, Culpeper, Crawshaw and Harrison 2008, Biber and Conrad 2019). The second one, "sociocultural" meaning, includes features associated with speaker identity categories, such as region, class, age, gender, ethnicity, dialect, and local culture, as studied in the three waves of variationist sociolinguistics (Eckert 2012). In the following paragraphs, we will illustrate each of these different categories. Before doing so, it

---

[26] Note that our use of the term 'use-conditional' meaning (instead of 'conventional non-truth-conditional meaning') is not a mere terminological quibble. We are strong advocates of defining concepts positively in terms of what they are (use conditions) rather than negatively in terms of what they are not (non-truth conditions).

is important to repeat that we do not conceive of semantics, pragmatics, and social meaning as discrete categories, which would potentially connote a modular approach to language. Our category-centred visualisation only serves an expository purpose. Ultimately, we consider these types of meaning to represent a gradient of linguistic knowledge with fuzzy boundaries (a view we explore further in terms of an 'expendability cline'), in line with usage-based cognitive principles.

Examples (45) to (51) will now be discussed to illustrate the distinctions introduced here at the level of use-conditional meaning. Examples (45) to (47) contain constructions that feature specific pragmatic properties.

(45) But it was almost, think wonderful, that they *were able to* discover this. (Leclercq and Depraetere 2022: 43)

(46) She thought, looking dubious. 'It doesn't sound likely. *Why should* there be a conspiracy?' (Cappelle, Depraetere and Lesuisse 2019: 231)

(47) What's that scratch doing on the table? (Kay and Fillmore 1999: 6)

Example (45) showcases the observation that the modal verb *be able to* is associated with an implicature of actualisation, whereby the event is construed as not only being possible but as having happened (Leclercq and Depraetere 2022). Implicatures are textbook cases of pragmatic information. It is also a specific pragmatic feature that distinguishes example (46). Here, though formulating a question, the speaker performs an expressive speech act by objecting to the content of the proposition expressed. Cappelle, Depraetere, and Lesuisse (2019: 231) argue that this speech act is conventionally associated with the '*Why should* ... ?' construction. Finally, another conventional pragmatic feature is exemplified in (47), which instantiates the '*What's* X *doing* Y?' construction. This construction, under the guise of a question, is used to indicate a speaker's judgement of incongruity regarding a particular situation (Kay and Fillmore 1999: 4).

Alternatively, the three examples (48) to (50) highlight social features of constructional meaning.

(48) ticker to delicious dishes built around the best foods for *cardio* health (Hilpert, Correia Saavedrea and Rains 2023: 29)

(49) I *didn't* do *nothing* (Hoffmann 2022: 241)

(50) dan wallace still a total twat then; *might can* get his teeth fixed with the £20 k he's totalled in price money. sorry jak if you read this (Morin, Desagulier and Grieve 2024: 24).

Example (48) showcases a feature relating to what we have called *interactional* social meaning: indeed, Hilpert, Correia Saavedra and Rains (2023: 35) have shown that register is a significant predictor for the choice of clippings (e.g., *cardio*) over their full source words (e.g., *cardiovascular*). Specifically, clippings tend to be used in registers of 'involved' text production as opposed to their full forms in 'informational' text production (Biber 1988), which is interpreted by the authors as constituting a meaning difference. We concur, and specifically we argue that it represents a social meaning difference in light of our proposed taxonomy. Secondly, in example (49) a *sociocultural* social meaning feature is considered. The utterance in this example instantiates the double negation construction, which Hoffmann (2022) revisits in the study of teenage speech in suburban Detroit schools by Eckert (2004), especially between the local communities of the Jocks (primarily middle-class teenagers) and the Burnouts (primarily working-class teenagers). Specifically, Hoffmann (2022: 241) analyses the double negation construction as including the social meaning features of 'positive local identity' and 'anti-school cool' stemming from the constructed sociolinguistic identity of the Burnouts. Thirdly, example (50) foregrounds a combination of interactional and sociocultural features of social meaning in constructional knowledge. The example includes an instance of the double modal construction *might can* in British English (Morin 2023), which has been shown to be strongly associated with the informal registers of English used on Twitter, as well as northern regions of the United Kingdom, especially the Scottish Borders (Morin, Desagulier and Grieve 2024). The authors argue that double modals such as *might can* are thus associated with social meaning features of 'register' and 'region', which distinguish such low-frequency constructions from more widespread, standard alternatives, e.g., *might be able to*.

In the last example, showcased in (51), Siewierska and Hollmann (2007) identify features that appear to be distributed across our taxonomy of use-conditional meanings.

(51) a. She gave him it.
      b. She gave it him. (Siewierska and Hollmann 2007: 87)

Biber et al. (2021: 920–921) show that the use of twin pronominal objects in the Dɪᴛʀᴀɴsɪᴛɪᴠᴇ construction is less common, with the Pʀᴇᴘᴏsɪᴛɪᴏɴᴀʟ Dᴀᴛɪᴠᴇ being the preferred form (i.e., *She gave it to him*). Pronominal sequences in the Dɪᴛʀᴀɴsɪᴛɪᴠᴇ construction are not impossible however. This is for instance the case in varieties of Northern English (see Siewierska and Hollmann 2007 and references cited therein). As shown in (51), two such sequences can be found. Either the recipient (*him*) precedes the theme (*it*), following the common ditransitive sequence with a nominal direct object (e.g., *She gave him the book*), as in (51a). Hughes and Trudgill (1996: 16) argue that this pattern can be found in southern varieties of British English. Or, as shown in (51b), the theme (*it*) can precede the recipient (*him*), which differs from the typical ditransitive sequence. Hughes and Trudgill (1996: 16) argue that this latter pattern can be found in northern varieties of British English, an observation which is confirmed by Siewierska and Hollmann (2007: 96) in their study of Lancashire English. This latter pattern interests us here for two reasons. First, theme-recipient twin pronoun ditransitives show a distinct information-structure contour from the more common recipient–theme sequence. This matters because it has potential implications for the pragmatic meaning of this construction: while the recipient-theme sequence of the DITRANSITIVE construction typically marks the recipient as the topic and the theme as the focus (Polinsky 1998), the theme-recipient sequence found in (51b) might instead be used to mark the theme as the topic and the recipient as the focus (given the relation, in the DITRANSITIVE construction, between focality and the end-weight principle, Goldberg 2014: 8). In addition to this pragmatic feature, (51b) also appears to be associated with a particular sociocultural social meaning, that of being a non-standard form of English that is regionally specific. Finally, because this pattern is shown by Biber et al. (2021: 21) to be most frequent in the register of conversation and fiction as opposed to news and academic, and because the first two of these registers are generally considered to be informal registers (though conversation more so than fiction, cf. Pisciotta 2024), an interactional social meaning feature of 'informal register' can also be specified as part of the meaning of the construction.

As a means of summarising examples 45–51, and to show that the framework of constructional meaning we propose is operationalised and can be implemented in future studies and descriptions of constructions, in Figure 5 we draw a formalised representation of the theme-initial variant of the twin pronoun ditransitive construction of (51b). This representation is broadly aligned with the annotational framework adopted by Hoffmann (2022) in a mainstream CxG

$$
\begin{array}{ll}
\text{FORM:} & \text{PHONOLOGY: } /A_1 \; B_2 \; C_3 \; D_4/_5 \\
& \text{MORPHOSYNTAX: } [\text{SUBJ}_1 \; [V_2 \; [\text{OBJ}_3]_{\text{ProN}} \; [\text{OBJ}_4]_{\text{ProN}}]_{\text{VP}}]_5 \\
\Leftrightarrow & \\
\text{MEANING:} & \text{SEMANTICS: 'CAUSE(EVENT}_2\text{(AGENT}_1\text{), RECEIVE(RECIPIENT}_3\text{, THEME}_4\text{))} \\
& \text{PRAGMATICS: TOPIC}_3 \; \text{FOCUS}_4 \\
& \text{SOCIAL: \; INTERACTIONAL: 'informal'}_5 \\
& \qquad\qquad \text{SOCIOCULTURAL: 'Northern British'}_5
\end{array}
$$

Figure 5 The TWO-PRONOUN THEME-INITIAL DITRANSITIVE (TTD) construction
(from Leclercq and Morin 2025).

approach, with a couple of tweaks. Firstly, as discussed in the previous paragraphs, the *pragmatics* level is now associated more narrowly with the utterance-focused side of use-conditional meaning, while the *social* level is now enriched by the two sub-levels of *interactional* and *socio-cultural*, i.e., the situational side of use-conditional meaning. This goes to show that the taxonomy developed here is not only descriptively useful, but can also aptly be formalised and operationalised, which is a central concern for many linguists. Figures 4 and 5 are proposals in this direction.

In conclusion to this section, we want to reflect upon the status of socio-pragmatic meaning in constructional knowledge. To be sure, cognitive and construction-based approaches to language have often expressed awareness of social dimensions of linguistic knowledge and use as a natural consequence of their foundational usage-based assumptions. In the broader cognitive linguistics literature, the assumption that meaning is experiential comprises the idea that social dimensions are part and parcel of our understanding of the world and thus our meaning structures (cf. quotes by Johnson 1987: xvi). A similar idea can be found more specifically in usage-based cognitive linguistics, and Langacker (1987: 63, 2008: 466–467, 2016: 469) is particularly consistent in this regard. We find him to be most explicit in the following quote:

> [T]he ground (the interlocutors, their interaction, and its circumstances) figures at least peripherally in the import of every unit. Indeed, abstracted units can incorporate any facet of the speech situation common to the usage events giving rise to them, such as the following: age, gender, and status of the interlocutors; their social relationship; nature of the occasion; degree of formality; attitudinal, emotive, and affective factors; and the language (or conceived linguistic variety) employed. (Langacker 2016: 469)

It is a similar stance that Bybee (2010: 14) adopts when arguing that social context provides a basis for the emergence of usage-based information. To some extent therefore, our proposal is only a continuation of this logic and mainly brings these assumptions to their descriptive consequences, but nevertheless we believe that such a framework should be fully engaged with in future CxG research. Indeed, the layers of meaning that we propose have not often been systematically modelled in construction-based approaches (Ungerer and Hartmann 2023: 44–45).[27] Only more recently can we find subtle references to features that we have explicitly identified as falling into

---

[27] One notable exception that Ungerer and Hartmann (2023) identify is Schmid's (2020) entrenchment-and-conventionalisation model, a cousin approach to CxG, in which he explicitly and consistently identifies socio-pragmatic features as part of the 'pragmatic associations' of a linguistic sign. See also Croft's (2001) identification of 'discourse-functional' meaning in constructions.

the socio-pragmatic domain, such as in Goldberg (2019: 94, emphasis added): 'lossy representations of language experience cluster together on various dimensions, including those related to form (phonology, grammatical categories, order, morphology) and function (meaning, *information structure, register, genre, dialect*)'.

In sum, the framework we propose here stems from predictions made by the theoretical assumptions of cognitive linguistics and CxG, but we believe that these predictions have been by and large overlooked in the CxG literature. Importantly, our argument is that such a framework is needed to be explicitly implemented as part of a 'social turn' for CxG (Morin 2023, unpublished[28], Morin, Desagulier and Grieve 2024), and that it should become a cornerstone of mainstream CxG from this point forward.

4.2 Interchangeability and Meaning Variation

The taxonomy of constructional meaning presented in Section 4.1 enables us not only to account for theoretical observations regarding the nature of linguistic knowledge, but also to shed light on thorny issues related to variation, the focus of this section.

While working separately on issues pertaining to pragmatics and social meaning, we felt the need to bring these dimensions together and establish the explicit taxonomy spelled out here when considering issues surrounding one of the 'auxiliary hypotheses' of CxG (Cappelle 2024: 7), namely *the principle of no synonymy*. The assumption of isomorphism in language predates the specific stance adopted in CxG, but it was formulated in the theory for the first time by Goldberg (1995):

> *The Principle of No Synonymy*: If two constructions are syntactically distinct, they must be semantically or pragmatically distinct (cf. Bolinger 1968; Haiman 1985; Clark 1987; MacWhinney 1989). Pragmatic aspects of constructions involve particulars of information structure, including topic and focus, and additionally stylistic aspects of the construction such as register. (Goldberg 1995: 67)

In the more recent literature, a number of different arguments have been put forward to question the accuracy of this principle. We provided counter-arguments to these in Leclercq and Morin (2023). While maintaining the core predictions of the principle, we agreed however that it would gain in precision and explanatory power by being reformulated under a new name, the principle of no equivalence:

---

[28] Book scheduled to be published with Oxford University Press in 2026.

> *The Principle of No Equivalence*: If two competing constructions differ in
> form (i.e. phonologically, morpho-syntactically or even orthographically),
> they must be semantically, pragmatically and/or socially distinct. (Leclercq
> and Morin 2023: 10)

Leclercq and Morin (2023: 10–12) highlight and explain the main changes that
needed to be made in order to fine-tune the principle (including the change of
name, why the term 'competition' was added, and the inclusion of phonological
and orthographic formal features). The detailed implications of the principle are
expounded in Leclercq, Morin, and Pijpops (unpublished), and two of these
implications are particularly relevant for us here.

First, applying our threefold taxonomy of meaning to this principle enables us
to identify all possible sources of variation that can be found between different
alternative constructions. Once again, while this may have been implicit in
previous constructionist research, it was important for us to pin down exactly
the meaning dimensions across which variation could take place (see Leclercq,
Morin and Pijpops (unpublished) for a detailed analysis). As mentioned in
Section 2.1.1, it is for instance a semantic feature that distinguishes the
DITRANSITIVE construction (e.g., *She gave my dad a book*) from the *to*-DATIVE
construction (e.g., *She gave a book to my dad*) and the *with*-APPLICATIVE construction (e.g., *She sprayed the wall with paint*) from the LOCATIVE CAUSED-MOTION
construction (e.g., *She sprayed paint on the wall*). Alternatively, it is a pragmatic
feature that distinguishes *can* and *could* from *be able to*, with only the latter form
being associated with an implicature of actualisation. Finally, alternative forms
such as *going to* and *gonna*, and *color* and *colour* show a difference in social
meaning, the first pair in terms of formal versus informal register (Mikkelsen and
Morin in press) and the second in terms of American versus British regional
variety (Leclercq, Morin and Pijpops unpublished). Interestingly, constructions
may differ in more than one of these dimensions: for example, the dative
alternation appears to involve all three levels at once (Leclercq, Morin and
Pijpops unpublished).

Second, we believe that the principle of no equivalence enables us to shed light
on a long-standing debate concerning the existence or prevalence of 'free variation' in alternations (Leino and Östman 2005, Cappelle 2009, Weber and Kopf
2023). This debate can be broken down into two sub-questions. To begin with,
a notable line of criticism levelled against the principle of no synonymy is that it is
incompatible with social types of linguistic variation. This has led Uhrig (2015:
331) to dub the principle one of 'no variation'. Specifically, the fear is that the
principle would contradict the Labovian assumption that language is rife with
'different ways of saying the same thing' (Labov 1972: 323). With 'no equivalence', however, it is guaranteed that sociolinguistic variation is compatible with

constructionist principles. The framing of the principle makes sure that the scope of isomorphism is not limited to semantics – which is the traditional focus of the term 'synonymy' (Ariel 2010: 28). That is to say, when one considers that synonymy is purely semantic, which is not Goldberg's (1995: 67) view (or ours), then 'no synonymy' indeed implies that speakers may never have different ways of expressing the same idea. By contrast, because no equivalence does not apply exclusively to semantics but can also specifically affect pragmatic or social meaning, the possibility for variation is safeguarded.[29] Indeed, the principle stipulates that any (but not necessarily all) of the three dimensions differ. This means, in practical terms, that two constructions may differ only in the social dimension. For instance, it is our understanding that a difference in social meaning is the sole feature that distinguishes, for example, *pop* from *soda* (region) and *buy* from *purchase* (register) (Goldberg 2019: 26). These two examples represent two distinct (social) ways of expressing the same (semantic) content. So instead of being excluded, sociolinguistic variation is in fact integrated with the principle of no equivalence. In addition, perhaps more strikingly, sociolinguistic variation is represented as being reflected *inside* constructional knowledge. In this respect, our model abides by Schmid's (2020: 309) critical observation that 'linguistic variation must not be regarded as an add-on to linguistic structure, but is instead part and parcel of it.'

The second sub-question evoked by the issue of free variation is that of optionality in the choice of constructional variants. For example, Cappelle (2009) considers the case of the alternation between two variants of particle placement: a 'joined' variant (e.g., *Don't just throw away that wrapper*) and a 'split' variant (e.g., *Don't just throw that wrapper away*) (Cappelle 2009: 2). While identifying a number of specific factors that predict the use of one or the other variant, Cappelle finds that in some cases speakers may also freely use either one, which thus questions the accuracy of the principle. At first sight, the phenomenon of optionality is not expected when assuming no equivalence, and may thus appear to constitute counter-evidence for it. We will shortly address factors that explain the contexts in which no equivalence appears to fail. Before doing so, we would like to focus on further reasons why, besides no equivalence, optionality comes out as a surprising result for us. There are in fact two additional reasons why optionality should be disfavoured. The first reason is theoretical: optionality is not an expected consequence of a foundational maxim underlying no equivalence, namely 'optimal expressivity' (Leclercq, Morin and

---

[29] Although a detailed discussion is beyond the scope of this Element, we would note that this conception of isomorphism (beyond the restricted domain of semantic meaning) also safeguards the possibility of language change and the compatibility between CxG and historical linguistics (see also Leclercq and Morin 2023: 10).

Pijpops unpublished). This maxim, inspired among others by the work of Zipf (1949) on *least effort* and Goldberg (1995: 67) on *maximised expressive power* and *maximised economy*, captures the observation that two opposing forces constrain the allotment of linguistic resources: while one would ideally dispose of a large range of expressions to express specific meanings (force one, 'communicative pressure for informativeness'), they also prefer to use existing means to convey a particular meaning (force two, 'cognitive pressure for linguistic simplicity'). Leclercq, Morin, and Pijpops (unpublished), using an agent-based simulation, show that this maxim is a cornerstone of no equivalence. The second reason, which quite naturally follows from the first, is cognitive:

> The fact that distinctions exist allows speakers to more quickly access the best match for their intended message-in-context when they speak. If two words were truly interchangeable, speakers would be forced to make a totally random decision each time either word was used. This would violate the efficiency aspect ... without contributing to expressiveness, since unbiased decisions take longer to make (Ratcliff et al., 2004) and yet contribute no additional information. (Goldberg 2019: 26)

In other words, it is reasonable to assume that optionality is cognitively costly and therefore dispreferred. Interestingly, Gardner et al. (2021) carried out a study of the cost of production based on a range of known grammatical variants in the literature (e.g., *that* versus *zero* complementizers, particle placement, dative alternation, *will* versus *be going to*). They found that the choice of a variant appears to be relatively effortless. In keeping with Goldberg (2019: 26), we view these findings as providing further support for no equivalence, for if the variants used were equivalent there should have been a cost in production efforts. Yet, this is not the conclusion drawn by Gardner et al. (2021). They argue instead that these results provide evidence against isomorphism and even conclude that language actually favours the availability of interchangeable expressions, a tendency labelled as the 'principle of optionality' by Van Hoey, Szmrecsanyi, and Gardner (unpublished[30]). To understand the authors' stance, it is crucial to appreciate their use of the terms 'variation' and 'variants' however. For indeed, they argue against a very strict version of isomorphism, whereby two forms cannot be *semantically* similar (Gardner et al. 2021: 8). We concur that total absence of semantic equivalence in language does not exist. However, this was not Goldberg's (1995: 67) claim in the principle of no synonymy, nor is it ours with the principle of no equivalence. As a matter of

---

[30] Van Hoey, T., Szmrecsanyi, B. & Gardner, M. H. Unpublished article entitled 'Language users don't mind optionality, and absolute complexity is not proportional to relative complexity'.

fact, all of the variants Gardner et al. (2021) study have been previously shown in the literature to display meaning differences across at least one of the three dimensions listed in Section 4.1, including in terms of semantics (see Cappelle 2009, Leclercq, Morin and Pijpops unpublished, Mikkelsen and Morin in press). So while the choice of these variants may not have been semantically motivated (and in that regard we are in agreement), they most certainly were pragmatically or socially motivated. We therefore disagree with Gardner et al. (2021: 30) when they conclude that linguists often consider 'that variation is unexpected, suboptimal, (needlessly) complex, and difficult for language users'. This might be the case for linguists who assume there can never be *semantic* interchangeability (i.e., the narrow acceptation of 'no synonymy'). With the principle of no equivalence, not only is variation considered possible, but it is also viewed as expected and effortless. In this respect, we therefore also disagree with De Smet (2019: 305) when he says that 'functionalists assume that variation is anomalous'.

We can now revisit cases of optionality in actual language use (where 'no equivalence' appears to be violated) with a fresh perspective. For indeed, we cannot ignore cases of free choice such as that of particle placement in English reported in Cappelle (2009). While we do not claim to have a definite answer, we attempt to provide a theoretical explanation of this phenomenon in the following paragraphs. This builds on the views developed in Leclercq, Morin, and Pijpops (unpublished) regarding the scope of the principle of no equivalence. To be clear, we maintain that those cases do not critically cast doubt on no equivalence. Instead, we believe that in such instances 'no equivalence' is overridden by external factors that clash with it. As a starting point, the principle makes predictions about *constructions*. 'No equivalence' is therefore to be understood as a cognitive disposition, and not as a rule that language users must obey. That is, it is at the level of entrenched, conventionalised units of the language that no equivalence is expected to occur, and not at the level of individual usage events. To establish such a distinction might come across as paradoxical or grotesque even, given the usage-based underpinnings of CxG, but we hope to clarify our view here. It is indeed one thing to posit a principle of constructional knowledge and another to account for the way it is observed in actual language use. There are two points in this regard that we consider need our attention.

The first major point to be made is that language production is not an idealised process (as is nicely captured, for example, by Reddy 1979 when critically discussing the conduit metaphor) whereby speakers can always retrieve and use any construction they want to communicate the specific meaning associated with them. For one, as discussed in Leclercq, Morin, and Pijpops unpublished, individual language use is influenced by various cognitive factors simultaneously. These factors include the preferences and abilities of the speaker (Wilson and Sperber 2002), communicative efficiency (Levshina 2022), linguistic processing speed (Christiansen and Chater 2016), and constraints on working memory due to stress, fatigue, and emotions (Blasiman and Was 2018). These competing demands on cognitive resources can lead to 'good-enough production' (Goldberg and Ferreira 2022), where the chosen forms may not perfectly convey the intended message. Goldberg and Ferreira (2022: 308) note that it is still unclear if speakers always fully grasp the function of a construction in such cases. While these contingencies are crucial for a complete understanding of cognition, they are beyond the scope of no equivalence.

The second major point relates to the types of pressures that constructional meaning exerts on speakers' choices. Much as speakers do not simply access and use specific constructions to convey specific meanings, as mentioned in Section 4.1, constructions do not simply make available meanings that are categorically encoded or not (a node-centred view), but constructional meanings are best viewed as more or less strongly linked to forms (a link-centred view). In our view, it is plausible to argue that meanings with strong links (whether semantic, pragmatic, or social) will be less amenable to being violated, compared to more weakly linked meanings, which might more easily be ignored by the speaker in choosing between alternative variants. Evidence tentatively supporting this view has recently been provided by Cai and De Smet (2024), who suggest that speakers' choices may be constrained by the cores of conceptual categories more so than by their peripheries. This means that any statistically significant bias, however large or small the effect is, falls in line with the principle of no equivalence. It remains, however, an open question what the minimal threshold is and how this threshold contributes to a speaker's choice. In addition to this, we would like to suggest that there might be what we would call an 'expendability cline' that is at play when determining the speaker's intended message. This cline follows naturally from the nature of the meaning types identified in the taxonomy. In simple terms, we believe that semantic meaning is less expendable than pragmatic meaning for this goal, which in turn is less expendable than social meaning. Regarding semantic meaning, we argue this is most likely to be true given the common intuition that 'truth-conditional' meaning plays a basic role in determining the content of an utterance. As shown in Figure 4, pragmatic meaning is also important in determining the content of an utterance, but plays a less basic role as it contributes to 'use-conditional' information, and is therefore more expendable than semantic meaning. Finally, we consider that social meaning is likely the most expendable of all three meaning types as it is less basic than both semantics and pragmatics; indeed, it does not directly contribute to the content of the 'utterance', but rather provides 'situational' information.[31] Of course, it is not our intention to imply that because a meaning feature type may be more expendable than another, it is less important than another. There are plenty of cases in which pragmatic meaning and social meaning will be the prime motivation of a speaker's choice (e.g., the implicature of actualisation in *be able to*, or the socially accommodated use of *trash* instead of *rubbish* by a native speaker of British English with their American flatmate), in which case they will hardly be expendable. However, our discussion here focuses on cases of good-enough production in which certain features are temporarily suspended by the speaker. Our claim is that when a speaker suspends (deliberately or not) certain features of meaning in choosing which constructions to use, certain features are more likely to be suspended than others, and that the tendency will be to safeguard semantic meaning. This, in our view, is the only way in which 'optionality' would seem to emerge in language use. However, in every other respect, besides the occasional by-product of (good-enough) production identified here, the principle of no equivalence as it applies to constructions is maintained.

4.3 Are Phonemes Meaningful?

Another dimension in which the taxonomy presented in Section 4.1 reveals itself to be useful and important for future CxG theorising is the question of elements that are generally considered to be non-symbolic, especially phonemes and phonotactic patterns.

Before addressing this specific topic, we should note that we are aware of the oft-cited issue of 'meaningless' constructions (see for instance Hilpert 2019: 50–57 and Cappelle 2024: 53–59 for overviews and references). As mentioned in the introduction though, we have adopted a mainstream approach to CxG, which assumes that there are no 'meaningless' constructions as such (Goldberg 2006: 166–182). Indeed, as pointed out by Cappelle (2024: 56), it is not 'easy to find structural patterns that the community of CxGians can all agree on are not associated with some kind of meaning'. That being said, there is one specific type of linguistic knowledge that is typically overlooked in constructional analysis, and that is phonemes and phonotactics:

> The one thing that CxG apparently has steered clear of until now is phonology
> (cf. Boas 2013: 239). To be sure, CxG in principle assumes a phonological

---

[31] The less basic status of social information has already been alluded to by Langacker (2016: 469), as he mentions that situational information in a usage event may be stored 'peripherally'

> form for all specific, i.e. filled, constructions or constructional components
> such as lexemes or morphemes, and particularly intonational patterns are often
> mentioned explicitly as parts of the phonological form of, say, utterance-level
> idiomatic constructions … Phonological elements themselves are, however,
> normally not thought of as constructions or included in constructional analysis.
> (Höder 2014: 204)

There may be a variety of reasons why phonemes and phonotactic patterns (henceforth 'phonological knowledge') are eschewed from constructional analysis, but one of them is certainly that these formal conventions do not appear to convey meaning. This is most problematic for a theory that posits form–meaning pairs 'all the way down' (Goldberg 2006: 18), and it raises a number of questions for which we aim to provide a tentative explanation.

The first question is to know, if phonological knowledge is indeed meaningless, whether the constructicon does in fact truly capture linguistic knowledge *in toto*. This is a challenge that may be engaged with in one of two ways. One way would be to explicitly acknowledge the possibility for linguistic knowledge to go beyond 'constructions' (i.e., form–meaning pairs) and to posit some sort of 'phonemicon' alongside the constructicon. We believe that this would create too big of a departure from the foundational premises of the theory however, as it would imply a modular view of language that is at odds with its usage-based assumptions. An easier solution, but no less radical, would be to argue that phonological knowledge does not exist beyond phonologically-specific constructions.[32] While this hypothesis echoes some proposals made in usage-based models (e.g., Langacker 2000, Bybee 2001), we agree with Nathan (2006) that it is not desirable and that there are good reasons to maintain the existence of abstract phonological knowledge.

The second question is to know whether phonological knowledge is indeed meaningless or whether it can be associated (to a lesser or greater degree) with particular meaning(s). While it may be tempting to answer the first part of this question positively (it is after all common ground in linguistics that *morphemes* are the smallest meaningful units of language), we believe there are reasons to consider alternative arguments. It is also common ground in linguistics that phonemes are in fact the smallest units of language capable of cueing meaning distinctions (for example, in the sense that /k/ and /b/ cue a difference in meaning between *cat* and *bat*). In the literature, this 'distinctive' role is assumed to constitute the function of phonological knowledge (Välimaa-Blum 2005: 57, Nesset 2008: 33, Höder 2014: 205–207). If one were to adopt a broad acceptation of the term *constructions* as symbolic associations of any 'form' and any

---

[32] This would be similar to Croft's (2001) position on parts of speech.

'function', this observation could be taken to suggest that phonological know-ledge is symbolic. However, this 'distinctive' function is subsidiary to the 'communicative intentions' that language users pursue when producing and perceiving utterances (Schmid 2020: 25), and it is our understanding that the mainstream definition of 'constructions' as form–meaning pairs typically focuses on said communicative intentions and not on distinctive functions. From this perspective, that phonemes serve a distinctive role still does not suffice for them to count as constructions per se (though see Morin (in press) for a critical discussion). For phonological elements to count as constructions, they would need to be associated with one or more of the meanings identified in Figure 4. Do they? There is some evidence suggesting that this is the case. First, the case of phonaesthemes (i.e., sub-morphemic 'sound–meaning pairings'; Bergen 2004: 290) is often cited as an exception to the meaninglessness of phonological knowledge (Höder 2014: 206; Schmid 2020: 292). Consider examples (52), (53), and (54):

(52) *gl-* 'light, vision' *glimmer, glisten, glitter, gleam, glow, glint,* etc. (Bergen 2004: 290)

(53) *-ack* 'abrupt decay' *clack, crack, whack, smack.* (adapted from Rhodes 1994: 280)

(54) *r-* 'irregular acoustic reference' *rattle, roll* [of thunder], *rip, racket.* (adapted from Rhodes 1994: 280)

These examples are meant to illustrate the observation that specific phono-logical elements can be associated with specific meanings. There are of course a number of critical observations that could be made about phonestheme theory (see, for example, Smith 2014: 17). It is for instance an empirical question how pervasive or exceptional a phenomenon this is (Blasi et al. 2016). The point remains though that specific phonological elements appear to be associated with specific meanings.[33] Besides this particular phenomenon, it could be argued that phonological elements generally lack any meaning though. We beg to disagree. In keeping with Schmid (2020: 292) and Hoffmann (2022), we would like to hypothesise that phonemes and phonotactic patterns readily convey social meaning.

Hoffmann (2022: 238–242) discusses several interesting examples of socially conditioned phonological variation that point in this direction, three of which we want to focus on here. First, referring to Labov's (1972) study on Martha's Vineyard, Hoffmann points out that the realisation of the diphthong in

---

[33] A much-discussed phenomenon related to phonaesthemes is known as the *bouba/kiki* effect, which places emphasis on the iconic nature of sound symbolism (see Fort and Schwartz 2022 for a recent discussion).

words such as *house* and *life* is deeply socially rooted. Instead of producing the Standard American English variants [haʊs] and [laɪf], Labov observed that a group of younger males also pronounced these words as [həʊs] and [ləɪf]. This is because these younger speakers were weary of mainland tourists and idolised local fishermen, whose pronunciation they adopted as 'they associated [it] with a positive social meaning of a "local Martha's Vineyard identity"' (Hoffmann 2022: 239). Next, Hoffmann discusses the pronunciation of <r> in pre-consonantal (/rC/) and final (r#) position. As shown in Labov (1972), rhoticity is a feature associated with the upper class (in 1960s New York English). Based on this observation, Hoffmann (2022: 238) draws a constructional template that singles out this identity marker as constituting the social meaning of rhoticity. Finally, Hoffmann refers to a study by Bell (1984) and discusses the realisation of intervocalic <t> in New Zealand English. Bell shows that in this variety of English speakers tend to voice intervocalic <t>, such that words like *writer* ['raetə'] are pronounced ['raet̬ə'], a feature which appears to index 'positive non-standard-identity' and which Hoffmann (2022: 242) annotates as the social meaning of this pattern.

Overall, this demonstration is meant to show that phonological knowledge is in fact imbued with social meaning. This observation is shared by Schmid (2020: 292), who also mentions that phonological variation readily conveys social meaning. Given the definition of 'constructions' endorsed earlier, the logical consequence is that all of these cases should be considered constructions in their own right. This is important because unlike the case of phonaesthemes, whose pervasiveness may be questionable or at least uncertain at this stage, it is a much better-established fact that phonology is inherently variable and especially indexes social stratifications (Foulkes 2021). In other words, we believe it is likely that many, if not most, phonological elements (i.e., phonemes and phonotactic patterns) are linked to particular social meanings. If this turns out to be true, the core constructionist assumption that the entirety of language is a network of constructions (i.e., form–meaning pairs) is preserved, as long as we establish a clear taxonomy of meaning which includes social information.[34]

5 Conclusion and Outlook

The general purpose of this Element was to offer a primer for the study of meaning in a CxG approach. It was structured along two main lines. The first three sections detailed the underlying assumptions regarding the nature of

---

[34] As Stefan Hartmann aptly pointed out to us, 'these considerations could partly be extended to written language, from the question of how the relationship between spoken and written language is, to aspects such as the social meaning of typography' (Stefan Hartmann, email to the authors, 13 September 2024).

meaning and the way it materialises in actual language use. Section 4 considered how meaning is modelled in construction-based research, and a revised framework was put forward to overcome a number of critical challenges.

While we strove to cover as much ground as possible, there remain a few topics that just barely exceeded the scope of this primer. One such topic concerns the lexicon–syntax continuum. As mentioned in the introduction, it is a core assumption in CxG that there is no dichotomy between a lexical module and a grammatical module. Does this mean that there is no strict distinction between lexical and grammatical meaning? This is generally what such a basic assumption is taken to imply. Yet it has been sporadically pondered whether, even in a non-modular approach, it would not be preferable to maintain a clear functional difference between lexical and grammatical constructions:

- While [grammatical] constructions are symbolic, one must not overlook the differences between lexemes and [grammatical] constructions. (Diessel 2019a: 107)
- Our study shows that while it may be so that grammar also carries meaning, some form-meaning pairings are privileged over others: those forms that constitute lexical items point to meanings that differ qualitatively from the meanings activated by forms that are traditionally considered grammatical. (Divjak et al. 2022: 26)
- One must not forget that although the form–meaning correspondence is indeed characteristic of both lexical and grammatical constructions, this is as far as the similarity goes between the different types of constructions. That is, even though *everything is a construction* in CxG, lexical and grammatical constructions remain located on opposite ends of the constructional continuum. . . . This does not challenge the view that both are form–meaning pairs but, rather, the assumption that they should capture the same type of meaning. (Leclercq 2024a: 158–159)

As mentioned in Section 3.3, it is sometimes assumed that lexical meaning is 'conceptual' while grammatical meaning is 'procedural'. In spite of this terminological difference, it remains unclear what distinguishes exactly lexical/conceptual meaning from grammatical/procedural meaning in CxG (see a critical discussion in Leclercq 2024a: 141–169). To address this point, Diessel (2019a: 108) discusses procedural meaning in terms of 'processing instructions', and Leclercq (2024a: 163) develops a view in terms of 'meta-concepts'. We decided against engaging this question in depth here, as it deviates from canonical constructionist assumptions and would require substantial space to do it justice. Our hope is that this question will be seriously taken up in future studies.

This Element was chiefly focused on the theoretical dimensions of meaning in CxG, but an exhaustive account would also need to incorporate methodological dimensions. For indeed, alongside its specific model of meaning, CxG relies on a range of empirical tools to analyse meaning. This is a topic that could well fill up an Element of its own. As Gries (2013: 93) points out, 'construction grammar . . . is probably one of the methodologically most pluralistic fields, as it utilizes a large number of different data and methodologies'. This includes corpus-based, experimental, and computational methods. Not only that, but the triangulation of methods is also largely endorsed by constructionist approaches (Ungerer and Hartmann 2023: 22). We concur with this epistemology, as shown in recent studies that have put to the test some of the theoretical dimensions unfolded in this Element. For example, Morin, Desagulier, and Grieve (2024) use a large social media corpus to study the social meaning of double modal constructions in British varieties of English. Likewise, Leclercq, Morin, and Pijpops (unpublished) make use of an agent-based computational simulation to test the predictions made by the principle of no equivalence. Future studies of this kind are expected to provide further insights into the model presented here. Notably, the 'expendability cline' proposed in Section 4.2 remains to be tested. We feel it is an experimental design involving human participants that is needed in this case, so as to explore the cognitive underpinnings of an effect likely conditioned by processing and production factors. This could be achieved using acceptability ratings, safe-paced reading tasks, eye-tracking, and more. Overall, and to conclude, such advanced methods make the application of a systematic framework of the meaning of constructions an exciting research programme for the future of construction grammar.

References

Anderson, S. (1971). On the role of deep structure in semantic interpretation. *Foundations of Language*, 7(3), 387–396.

Ariel, M. (2010). *Defining Pragmatics*. Cambridge: Cambridge University Press.

Ariel, M. (2023). A usage-based analysis of the semantics/pragmatics interface. In T. Li, ed., *Handbook of Cognitive Semantics*. Leiden: Brill, pp. 269–297.

Auf der Strasse, A. (2017). *Constructions in Use*. Düsseldorf: Düsseldorf University Press.

Austin, J. L. (1962). *How To Do Things with Words*. Oxford: Clarendon Press.

Barðdal, J. (2008). *Productivity: Evidence from Case and Argument Structure in Icelandic*. Amsterdam: John Benjamins.

Beckner, C., Blythe, R., Bybee, J., Christiansen, M., Croft, W., Ellis, N., Holland, J., Ke, J., Larsen-Freeman, D. & Schoenemann, T. (2009). Language is a complex-adaptive system: Position paper. *Language Learning*, 59(1), 1–26.

Bell, A. (1984). Language style as audience design. *Language in Society*, 13(2), 145–204.

Bergen, B. (2004). The psychological reality of phonaesthemes. *Language*, 80(2), 290–311.

Bergen, B. (2016). Embodiment, simulation and meaning. In N. Riemer, ed., *Routledge Handbook of Semantics*. Abingdon: Routledge, pp. 142–157.

Bergen, B. & Chang, N. (2013). Embodied Construction Grammar. In T. Hoffmann & G. Trousdale, eds., *The Oxford Handbook of Construction Grammar*. Oxford: Oxford University Press, pp. 168–190.

Bergs, A. (2018). Learn the rules like a pro, so you can break them like an artist (Picasso): Linguistic aberrancy from a constructional perspective. *Zeitschrift für Anglistik und Amerikanistik*, 66(3), 277–293.

Bergs, A. (2019). What, if anything, is linguistic creativity? *Gestalt Theory*, 41(2), 173–183.

Bergs, A. & Kompa, N. A. (2020). Creativity within and outside the linguistic system. *Cognitive Semiotics*, 13, 20202025.

Biber, D. (1988). *Variation Across Speech and Writing*. Cambridge: Cambridge University Press.

Biber, D. & Conrad, S. (2019). *Register, Genre, and Style*, 2nd ed. Cambridge: Cambridge University Press.

Biber, D., Johannsson, S., Leech, G. N., Conrad, S., Finegan, E. & Quirk, R. (2021). *Grammar of Spoken and Written English*. Amsterdam: John Benjamins.

Blasi, D., Wichmann, W., Hammarström, H., Stadler, P. & Christiansen, M. (2016). Sound-meaning association biases evidenced across thousands of languages. *Proceedings of National Academy of Sciences*, 113(39), 10818–10823.

Blasiman, R. N. & Was, C. A. (2018). Why is working memory performance unstable? A review of 21 factors. *Europe's Journal of Psychology*, 14(1), 188–231.

Boas, H. C. (2011). Coercion and leaking argument structures in Construction Grammar. *Linguistics*, 49(6), 1271–1303.

Boas, H. C. (2013). Cognitive construction grammar. In T. Hoffmann & G. Trousdale, eds., *The Oxford Handbook of Construction Grammar*. Oxford: Oxford University Press, pp. 233–254.

Boas, H. (2021). Construction grammar and frame semantics. In X. Wen & J. Taylor, eds., *The Routledge Handbook of Cognitive Linguistics*. New York: Routledge, pp. 43–77.

Boas, H. (in press). What happened to Frame Semantics? *English Linguistics*

Boas, H., Leino, J. & Lyngfelt, B. (2024). Constructionist views on construction grammar. *Constructions and Frames*, 16(2), 169–190.

Bolinger, D. (1968). Entailment and the meaning of structures. *Glossa*, 2, 119–127.

Booij, G. (2010). *Construction Morphology*. Oxford: Oxford University Press.

Boyd, J. & Goldberg, A. E. (2011). Learning what not to say: The role of statistical pre-emption and categorization in "a"-adjective production. *Language*, 81, 1–29.

Boye, K. & Harder, P. (2012). A usage-based theory of grammatical status and grammaticalization. *Language*, 88(1), 1–44.

Brdar, M. (2018). Novel metonymies, wine and wineskins, old and new ones. In S. Gudurić & B. Radić-Bojanić, eds., *Jezici i kulture u vremenu i prostoru VII/1*. Novi Sad: Filozofski fakultet/Pedagoško društvo Vojvodine, pp. 123–134.

Breban, T. (2014). What is secondary grammaticalization? Trying to see the wood for the trees in a confusion of interpretations. *Folia Linguistica*, 48(2), 469–502.

Brems, L. (2011). *The Layering of Size and Type Noun Constructions in English*. Berlin: Mouton de Gruyter.

Brems, L. (2012). The establishment of quantifier constructions for size nouns: A diachronic study of heap(s) and lot(s). *Journal of Historical Pragmatics*, 13, 202–231.

Brône, G. (2017). Cognitive linguistics and humor research. In S. Attardo, ed., *The Routledge Handbook of Language and Humor*. New York: Routledge, pp. 250–266.

Budts, S. & Petré, P. (2016). Reading the intentions of *be going to*: On the subjectification of future markers. *Folia Linguistica*, 50, 1–32.

Busso, L., Perek, F. & Lenci, A. (2021). Constructional associations trump lexical associations in processing valency coercion. *Cognitive Linguistics*, 32(2), 287–318.

Bybee, J. (2001). *Phonology and Language Use*. Cambridge: Cambridge University Press.

Bybee, J. (2006a). From usage to grammar: The mind's response to repetition. *Language*, 82(4), 711–733.

Bybee, J. (2006b). Language change and universals. In R. Mairal & J. Gil, eds., *Linguistic Universals*. Cambridge: Cambridge University Press, pp. 179–194.

Bybee, J. (2010). *Language, Usage, and Cognition*. Cambridge: Cambridge University Press.

Bybee, J. (2013). Usage-based theory and exemplar representations of constructions. In T. Hoffmann & G. Trousdale, eds., *The Oxford Handbook of Construction Grammar*. Oxford: Oxford University Press, pp. 49–69.

Cai, Y. & De Smet, H. (2024). Are categories' cores more isomorphic than their peripheries? *Frontiers in Communication*, 9, 1310234.

Cappelle, B. (2009). Can we factor out free choice? In A. Dufte, J. Fleischer & G. Seiler eds., *Describing and Modeling Variation in Grammar*. Berlin: Mouton de Gruyter, pp. 183–202.

Cappelle, B. (2017). What's pragmatics doing outside constructions? In I. Depraetere & R. Salkie, eds., *Semantics and Pragmatics: Drawing a Line*. Berlin: Springer, pp. 115–151.

Cappelle, B. (2020). Playing by/with the rules: Creativity in language, games, and art. *Cognitive Semiotics*, 13(1), 1–8. doi.org/10.1515/cogsem-2020-2026.

Cappelle, B. (2024). *Can Construction Grammar Be Proven Wrong?* Cambridge: Cambridge University Press.

Cappelle, B. & Depraetere, I. (2016). Short-circuited interpretations of modal verb constructions: Some evidence from *The Simpsons*. *Constructions and Frames*, 8(1), 7–39.

Cappelle, B., Depraetere, I. & Lesuisse, M. (2019). The necessity modals *have to*, *must*, *need to*, and *should*: Using n-grams to help identify common and distinct semantic and pragmatic aspects. *Constructions and Frames*, 11(2), 220–243.

Carston, R. (2010). Truth-conditional semantics. In J.-O. Östman, M. Sbisà & J. Verschueren, eds., *Philosophical Perspectives for Pragmatics*. Amsterdam: John Benjamins, pp. 280–288.

Chomsky, N. (1957). *Syntactic Structures*. The Hague: Mouton and Co.

Chomsky, N. (1965). *Aspects of the Theory of Syntax*. Cambridge, MA: The MIT Press.

Chomsky, N. (1971). Deep structure, surface structure, and semantic interpretation. In D. Steinberg & L. Jacobovits, eds., *Semantics*. London: London University Press, pp. 183–216.

Christiansen, M. H. & Chater, N. (2016). The now-or-never bottleneck: A fundamental constraint on language. *Behavioral and Brain Sciences*, 39, e62.

Clark, E. (1987). The principle of contrast: A constraint on language acquisition. In B. MacWhinney, ed., *Mechanisms of Language Acquisition*. Hillsdale: Lawrence Erlbaum Associates, pp. 1–33.

Coussé, E., Andersson, P. & Olofsson, J. (2018a). Grammaticalization meets construction grammar: Opportunities, challenges and potential incompatibilities. In E. Coussé, P. Andersson & J. Olofsson, eds., *Grammaticalization Meets Construction Grammar*. Amsterdam: John Benjamins, pp. 3–19.

Coussé, E., Andersson, P. & Olofsson, J. (2018b). *Grammaticalization Meets Construction Grammar*. Amsterdam: John Benjamins.

Croft, W. (2001). *Radical Construction Grammar: Syntactic Theory in Typological Perspective*. Oxford: Oxford University Press.

Croft, W. (2009). Toward a social cognitive linguistics. In V. Evans & S. Pourcel, eds., *New Directions in Cognitive Science*. Amsterdam: John Benjamins, pp. 395–420.

Croft, W. & Cruse, D. A. (2004). *Cognitive Linguistics*. Cambridge: Cambridge University Press.

Culpeper, J. (2021). Sociopragmatics. In M. Haugh, D. Kadar & M. Terkourafi, eds., *The Cambridge Handbook of Sociopragmatics*. Cambridge: Cambridge University Press, pp. 15–29.

Culpeper, J., Crawshaw, R. & Harrison, J. (2008). 'Activity types' and 'discourse types': Mediating 'advice' in interactions between foreign language assistants and their supervisors in schools in France and England. *Multilingua*, 27, 297–324.

Cuyckens, H. (2018). Reconciling older and newer approaches to grammaticalization. *Yearbook of the Cognitive Linguistics Association*, 6, 183–196.

Daugs, R. (2023). *Modality, usage and diachrony: Constructional changes in the modal domain in American English*. PhD thesis, Christian-Albrechts-Universität, Kiel.

Davies, M. (2008-). *The Corpus of Contemporary American English (COCA)*. Available online at www.english-corpora.org/coca/.

Dawson, H. C. & Phelan, M. (2016). *The Language Files: Materials for an Introduction to Language and Linguistics*. Columbus, OH: Ohio State University Press.

Desagulier, G. & Monneret, P. (2023). Cognitive linguistics and a usage-based approach to the study of semantics and pragmatics. In M. Díaz-Campos & S. Balasch, eds., *The Handbook of Usage-Based Linguistics*. Hoboken, NJ: Wiley-Blackwell, pp. 31–53.

De Smet, H. (2019). The motivated unmotivated: Variation, function and context. In K. Bech & R. Möhlig-Falke, eds., *Grammar – Discourse – Context: Grammar and Usage in Language Variation and Change*. Berlin: Mouton de Gruyter, pp. 305–332.

Diessel, H. (2007). Frequency effects in language acquisition, language use, and diachronic change. *New Ideas in Psychology*, 25, 108–127.

Diessel, H. (2019a). *The Grammar Network: How Linguistic Structure is Shaped by Language Use*. Cambridge: Cambridge University Press.

Diessel, H. (2019b). Usage-based construction grammar. In E. Dąbrowska & D. Divjak, eds., *Cognitive Linguistics: A Survey of Linguistic Subfields*. Berlin: Mouton de Gruyter, pp. 50–80.

Diessel, H. (2023). *The Constructicon*. Cambridge: Cambridge University Press.

Diewald, G. (2011). Pragmaticalization (defined) as grammaticalization of discourse functions. *Linguistics*, 49(2), 365–390.

Divjak, D., Milin, P. & Medimorec, S. (2020). Construal in language: A visual-world approach to the effects of linguistic alternations on event perception and conception. *Cognitive Linguistics*, 31(1), 37–72.

Divjak, D., Milin, P., Medimorec, S. & Borowski, M. (2022). Behavioral signatures of memory resources for language: Looking beyond the lexicon/ grammar divide. *Cognitive Science*, 46, e13206.

Eckert, P. (2004). Adolescent language. In E. Finnegan & J. Rickford, eds., *Language in the USA*. Cambridge: Cambridge University Press, pp. 251–289.

Eckert, P. (2012). Three waves of variation study: The emergence of meaning in the study of sociolinguistic variation. *Annual Review of Anthropology*, 41, 87–100.

Evans, V. (2006). Lexical concepts, cognitive models and meaning-construction. *Cognitive Linguistics*, 17(4), 491–534.

Evans, V. (2012). Cognitive Linguistics. *WIREs Cognitive Science*, 3(2), 129–141.

Evans, V. & Green, M. (2006). *Cognitive Linguistics: An Introduction*. Edinburgh: Edinburgh University Press.

Fauconnier, G. (1994). *Mental Spaces: Aspects of Meaning Construction in Natural Language*. Cambridge: Cambridge University Press.

Fauconnier, G. (1997). *Mappings in Thought and Language*. Cambridge: Cambridge University Press.

Fauconnier, G. (2001). Conceptual blending and analogy. In D. Gentner, K. J. Holyoak & B. N. Kokinov, eds., *The Analogical Mind: Perspectives from Cognitive Science*. Cambridge, MA: The MIT Press, pp. 255–285.

Fauconnier G. & Turner, M. (1996). Blending as a Central Process of Grammar. In A. E. Goldberg, ed., *Conceptual Structure, Discourse, and Language*. Stanford, CA: CSLI, pp. 113–129.

Fauconnier, G. & Turner, M. (1998). Conceptual integration networks. *Cognitive Science*, 22(2), 133–187.

Fauconnier, G. & Turner, M. (2008). *The Way We Think: Conceptual Blending and the Mind's Hidden Complexities*. New York: Basic Books.

Fillmore, C. J. (1982). Frame semantics. In Linguistic Society of Korea, ed., *Linguistics in the Morning Calm*. Seoul: Hanshin, pp. 111–138.

Fillmore, C. J. (1985). Frames and the semantics of understanding. *Quaderni di Semantica*, 6, 222–253.

Fillmore, C. J. (2006). Frame semantics. In D. Geeraerts, ed., *Cognitive Linguistics: Basic Readings*. Berlin: Mouton de Gruyter, pp. 373–400.

Finkbeiner, R. (2019). Reflections on the role of pragmatics in construction grammar. *Constructions and Frames*, 11(2), 171–192.

Foolen, A. (2023). Construction pragmatics in a wider context: An addition to Wen (2022). *Lege Artis. Language Yesterday, Today, Tomorrow*, 8(1), 21–31.

Fort, M. & Schwartz, J-L. (2022). Resolving the bouba-kiki effect by rotting iconic sound symbolism in physical properties of round and spiky objects. *Scientific Reports*, 12, 1–12.

Foulkes, P. (2021). Phonological variation: A global perspective. In B. Aarts, A. McMahon & L. Hinrichs, eds., *The Handbook of English Linguistics*, 2nd ed. Hoboken, NJ: Wiley, pp. 625–669.

Gärdenfors, P. (1999). Some tenets of cognitive semantics. In J. S. Allwood & P. Gärdenfors, eds., *Cognitive Semantics: Meaning and Cognition*. Amsterdam: John Benjamins, pp. 19–36.

Gardner, M. H., Uffing, E., Van Vaeck, N. & Szmrecsanyi, B. (2021). Variation isn't that hard: Morphosyntactic choice does not predict production difficulty. *PLoS ONE*, 16(6), e0252602.

Geeraerts, D. (2010). *Theories of Lexical Semantics*. Oxford: Oxford University Press.

Geeraerts, D. & Cuyckens, H., eds. (2007). *The Oxford Handbook of Cognitive Linguistics*. Oxford: Oxford University Press.

Gildea, S. & Barðdal, J. (2023). From grammaticalization to diachronic construction grammar: A natural evolution of the paradigm. *Studies in Language*, 47(4), 743–788.

Givón, T. (1991). The evolution of dependent clause morpho-syntax in biblical Hebrew. In E. C. Traugott & B. Heine, eds., *Approaches to Grammaticalization*, vol. 2, *Types of Grammatical Markers*. Amsterdam: John Benjamins, pp. 257–310.

Glynn, D. (2022). Emergent categories: Quantifying analogically derived similarity in usage. In K. Krawczak, M. Grygiel & B. Lewandowska-Tomaszczyk, eds., *Analogy and Contrast in Language*. Amsterdam: John Benjamins, pp. 246–282.

Goldberg, A. E. (1995). *Constructions: A Construction Grammar Approach to Argument Structure*. Chicago, IL: University of Chicago Press.

Goldberg, A. E. (2002). Surface generalizations: an alternative to alternations. *Cognitive Linguistics*, 13, 327–356.

Goldberg, A. E. (2004). Pragmatics and argument structure. In L. R. Horn & G. L. Ward, eds., *The Handbook of Pragmatics*. Oxford: Blackwell, pp. 427–441.

Goldberg, A. E. (2006). *Constructions at Work: The Nature of Generalization in Language*. Oxford: Oxford University Press.

Goldberg, A. E. (2013). Constructionist approaches. In T. Hoffmann & G. Trousdale, eds., *The Oxford Handbook of Construction Grammar*. Oxford: Oxford University Press, pp. 14–31.

Goldberg, A. E. (2014). The information structure of ditransitives: informing scope properties and long-distance dependency constraints. In S. Katz Bourns & L. L. Myers, eds., *Perspectives on Linguistic Structure and Context: Studies in Honour of Knud Lambrecht*, Amsterdam: John Benjamins, pp. 3–16.

Goldberg, A. E. (2016). Partial productivity of linguistic constructions: Dynamic categorization and statistical preemption. *Language and Cognition*, 8(3), 369–390.

Goldberg, A. E. (2019). *Explain Me This: Creativity, Competition, and the Partial Productivity of Constructions*. Princeton, NJ: Princeton University Press.

Goldberg, A. E. & Ferreira, F. (2022). Good-enough language production. *Trends in Cognitive Sciences*, 26(4), 300–11.

Goldberg, A. E. & Shirtz, S. (in press). The English phrase-as-lemma construction: When a phrase masquerades as a word, people play along. *Language*.

Gonzalves-Garcia, F. (2020). Maximizing the explanatory power of constructions in cognitive construction grammar(s). *Belgian Journal of Linguistics*, 34, 110–121.

Goossens, L. (1990). Metaphtonymy: The interaction of metaphor and metonymy in expressions for linguistic action. *Cognitive Linguistics*, 1–3, 323–340.

Grady, J., Oakley, T. & Coulson, S. (1999). Blending and metaphor. In G. Steen & R. Gibbs, eds., *Metaphor in Cognitive Linguistics*. Amsterdam: John Benjamins, pp. 101–124.

Gries, S. (2013). Data in construction grammar. In T. Hoffmann, & G. Trousdale, eds., *The Oxford Handbook of Construction Grammar*. Oxford: Oxford University Press, pp. 93–108.

Gutzmann, D. (2015). *Use-Conditional Meaning: Studies in Multidimensional Semantics*. Oxford: Oxford University Press.

Haiman, J. (1985). *Natural Syntax: Iconicity and Erosion*. Cambridge: Cambridge University Press.

Hall-Lew, L., Moore, E. & Podesva, R. (2021). Social meaning and linguistic variation: Theoretical foundations. In L. Hall-Lew, E. Moore & R. Podesva, eds., *Social Meaning and Linguistic Variation: Theorizing the Third Wave*. Cambridge: Cambridge University Press, pp. 1–24.

Harris, R. A. (1993). *The Linguistics Wars*. Oxford: Oxford University Press.

Harris, R. A. (2022). *The Linguistics Wars: Chomsky, Lakoff, and the Battle over Deep Structure*, 2nd ed. Oxford: Oxford University Press.

Hartmann, S. & Ungerer, T. (2023). Attack of the snowclones: A corpus-based analysis of extravagant formulaic patterns. *Journal of Linguistics*, 30(3), 599–634. doi.org/10.1017/S0022226723000117.

Haspelmath, M. (1999). Why is grammaticalization irreversible? *Linguistics*, 37(6), 1043–1068.

Herbst, T. & Hoffmann, T. (2018). Construction grammar for students: A constructionist approach to syntactic analysis (CASA). *Yearbook of the German Cognitive Linguistics Association*, 6(1), 197–218.

Herbst, T. & Hoffmann, T. (2024). *A Construction Grammar of the English Language: CASA – A Constructionist Approach to Syntactic Analysis*. Amsterdam: John Benjamins.

Hilpert, M. (2016). Change in modal meanings: Another look at the shifting collocates of may. *Constructions and Frames*, 8(1), 66–85.

Hilpert, M. (2018). Three open questions in diachronic construction grammar. In E. Coussé, P. Andersson & J. Olofsson, eds., *Grammaticalization Meets Construction Grammar*. Amsterdam: John Benjamins, pp. 21–39.

Hilpert, M. (2019). *Construction Grammar and its Application to English*, 2nd ed. Edinburgh: Edinburgh University Press.

Hilpert, M. (2021). *Ten Lectures on Diachronic Construction Grammar*. Leiden & Boston: Brill.

Hilpert, M. & Flach, S. (2023). Modals in the network model of construction grammar. In I. Depraetere, B. Cappelle, M. Hilpert et al., eds., *Models of Modals: From Pragmatics and Corpus Linguistics to Machine Learning*. Berlin: Mouton de Gruyter, pp. 254–270.

Hilpert, M, Correia Saavedra, D. & Rains, J. (2023). Meaning differences between English clippings and their source words: a corpus-based study. *ICAME Journal*, 47(1), 19–37.

Höder, S. (2014). Phonological Elements and Diasystematic Construction Grammar. *Constructions and Frames*, 6(2), 202–231.

Hoffmann, T. (2020a). Construction grammar and creativity: evolution, psychology, and cognitive science. *Cognitive Semiotics*, 13(1), 1–11.

Hoffmann, T. (2020b). Speakers are creative, within limits: A response to Peter Uhrig. *Cognitive Semiotics*, 13(1), 1–7.

Hoffmann T. (2021). Multimodal construction grammar: From multimodal constructs to multimodal constructions. In X. Wen & J. Taylor, eds., *The Routledge Handbook of Cognitive Linguistics*. New York: Routledge, pp. 78–92.

Hoffmann, T. (2022). *Construction Grammar: The Structure of English*. Cambridge: Cambridge University Press.

Hoffmann, T. (in press). Cognitive approaches to linguistic creativity. In X. Wen & C. Sinha, eds., *The Cambridge Encyclopedia of Cognitive Linguistics*. Cambridge: Cambridge University Press.

Hoffmann, T. & Trousdale, G. (2013). *The Oxford Handbook of Construction Grammar*. Oxford: Oxford University Press.

Hopper, P. & Traugott, E. C. (2003). *Grammaticalization*. Cambridge: Cambridge University Press.

Horn, L. (1985). Metalinguistic negation and pragmatic ambiguity. *Language*, 61(1), 121–174.

Huang, Y. (2014). *Pragmatics*, 2nd ed. Oxford: Oxford University Press.

Huck, G. & Goldsmith, J. (1996). *Ideology and Linguistic Theory: Noam Chomsky and the Deep Structure Debates*. London: Routledge.

Hugues, A. & Trudgill, P. (1996). *English Accents and Dialects: An Introduction to the Social and Regional Varieties of English in the British Isles*, 3rd ed. London: Arnold.

Israel, M. (1996). The way constructions grow. In A. E. Goldberg, ed., *Conceptual Structure, Discourse and Language*. Stanford, CA: CSLI, pp. 217–230.

Johnson, M. (1987). *The Body in the Mind: The Bodily Basis of Meaning, Imagination, and Reason*. Chicago, IL: University of Chicago Press.

Joseph, B. (1992). Yet more on -gate words: a perspective from Greece. *American Speech*, 67(2), 222–223.

Joseph, B. (1998). Diachronic morphology. In A. Spencer & A. Zwicky, eds., *The Handbook of Morphology*. Oxford: Blackwell, pp. 349–373.

Jurafsky, D. (1992). *An on-line computational model of human sentence interpretation: A theory of the representation and use of linguistic knowledge.* PhD thesis, University of California, Berkeley.

Kapatsinski, V. (2023). Understanding the roles of type and token frequency in usage-based linguistics. In M. Díaz-Campos & S. Balasch, eds., *The Handbook of Usage-Based Linguistics*. Wiley: New Jersey, pp. 91–106.

Kasper, S. & Purschke, C. (2023). Whatever happened to the scene-encoding hypothesis? Salience and pertinence as the missing links between the usage-based model and scene encoding. *Constructions*, 15, 1–22.

Katz, J. & Postal, P. (1964). *An Integrated Theory of Linguistic Descriptions*. Cambridge, MA: The MIT Press.

Kay, P. (2004). Pragmatic aspects of grammatical constructions. In L. R. Horn & G. Ward, eds., *Handbook of Pragmatics*. Oxford: Blackwell, pp. 675–700.

Kay, P. & Fillmore, C. (1999). Grammatical constructions and linguistic generalizations: The What's X doing Y? construction. *Language*, 75(1), 1–33.

Kay, P. & Michaelis, L. A. (2012). Constructional meaning and compositionality. In C. Maienborn, K. Heusinger & P. Portner, eds., *Semantics: An International Handbook of Natural Language Meaning*, vol. 3. Berlin: Mouton de Gruyter, pp. 2271–2296.

Kay P. & Michaelis, L. A. (2019). Constructional meaning and compositionality. In C. Maienborn, K. Heusinger & P. Portner, e ds., *Semantics – Interfaces*. Berlin: Mouton de Gruyter, pp. 293–324.

Keller, R. (1994). *Sprachwandel: Von der unsichtbaren Hand in der Sprache*. Tübingen & Basel: Francke.

Kövecses, Z. (2006). *Language, Mind and Culture: A Practical Introduction*. Oxford: Oxford University Press.

Kranich, S. (2008). Subjective progressives in seventeenth and eighteenth century English: Secondary grammaticalization as a process of objectification. In M. Gotti, M. Dossena & R. Dury, eds., *English Historical Linguistics 2006*, vol. I, *Syntax and Morphology*. Amsterdam: John Benjamins, pp. 241–256.

Kranich, S. (2010). Grammaticalization, subjectification and objectification. In K. Stathi, E. Gehweiler & E. König, eds., *Grammaticalization: Current Views and Issues*. Amsterdam: John Benjamins, pp. 101–121.

Krug, M. G. (2000). *Emerging English Modals*. Berlin: Mouton de Gruyter.

Kuryłowicz, J. (1965). The evolution of grammatical categories. *Diogenes*, 55–71.

Kuzai, E. (2020). Pragmatic information in constructions: What do speakers generalize? *Belgian Journal of Linguistics*, 34, 215–227.

Labov, W. (1972). *Sociolinguistic Patterns*. Philadelphia: University of Pennsylvania Press.

Lakoff, G. (1973). Hedges: A study in the meaning criteria and the logic of fuzzy concepts. *Journal of Philosophical Logic*, 2, 458–508.

Lakoff, G. (1987). *Women, Fire, and Dangerous Things: What Categories Reveal About the Mind*. Chicago: Chicago University Press.

Lakoff, G. (1988). Cognitive semantics. In U. Eco, M. Santambrogio & P. Violi, eds., *Meaning and Mental Representations*. Bloomington, IN: Indiana University Press, pp. 119–154.

Lakoff, G. (1993). The contemporary theory of metaphor. In A. Ortony, ed., *Metaphor and Thought*. Cambridge: Cambridge University Press, pp. 202–251.

Lakoff, G. & Johnson, M. (1980). *Metaphors We Live By*. Chicago: Chicago University Press.

Langacker, R. W. (1987). *Foundations of Cognitive Grammar*, vol. 1, *Theoretical Prerequisites*. Stanford, CA: Stanford University Press.

Langacker, R. W. (1990). Subjectification. *Cognitive Linguistics*, 1, 5–38.

Langacker, R. W. (1991). *Foundations of Cognitive Grammar*, vol. 2, *Descriptive Application*. Stanford, CA: Stanford University Press.

Langacker, R. W. (2000). A dynamic usage-based model. In M. Barlow & S. Kemmer, eds., *Usage-Based Models of Language*. Stanford, CA: CSLI, pp. 1–63.

Langacker, R. W. (2005). Construction grammars: Cognitive, radical, and less so. In F. J. Ruiz de Mendoza Ibáñez & M. Sandra Peña Cervel, eds., *Cognitive Linguistics: Internal Dynamics and Interdisciplinary Interaction*. Berlin: Mouton de Gruyter, pp. 101–159.

Langacker, R. W. (2008). *Cognitive Grammar: A Basic Introduction*. Oxford: Oxford University Press.

Langacker, R. W. (2010). *Concept, Image, Symbol: The Cognitive Basis of Grammar*. Berlin: Mouton de Gruyter.

Langacker, R. W. (2011). Grammaticalization and Cognitive Grammar. In H. Narrog & B. Heine, eds., *The Oxford Handbook of Grammaticalization*. Oxford: Oxford University Press, pp. 79–91.

Langacker, R. W. (2016). Working towards a synthesis. *Cognitive Linguistics*, 27(4), 465–77.

Leclercq, B. (2019). Coercion: A case of saturation. *Constructions and Frames*, 11(2), 270–289.

Leclercq, B. (2020). Semantics and pragmatics in construction crammar. *Belgian Journal of Linguistics*, 34, 225–234.

Leclercq, B. (2023a). Ad hoc concepts and the relevance heuristics: A false paradox? *Pragmatics*, 33(3), 324–342.

Leclercq, B. (2023b). Modality revisited: Combining insights from construction grammar and relevance theory. In I. Depraetere, B. Cappelle & M. Hilpert et al., eds., *Models of Modals: From Pragmatics and Corpus Linguistics to Machine Learning*. Berlin: Mouton de Gruyter, pp. 60–92.

Leclercq, B. (2024a). *Linguistic Knowledge and Language Use: Bridging Construction Grammar and Relevance Theory*. Cambridge: Cambridge University Press.

Leclercq, B. (2024b). The post-modal grammaticalisation of concessive *may* and *might*. *Constructions and Frames*, 16(1), 130–161.

Leclercq, B. (2024c). The semantics–pragmatics interface in construction grammar. In H. Nesi & P. Milin, eds., *International Encyclopedia of Language and Linguistics*, 3rd ed. Online First, pp. 1–4.

Leclercq, B. & Depraetere, I. (2022). Making meaning with *be able to*: modality and actualisation. *English Language and Linguistics*, 26(1), 27–48.

Leclercq, B. & Morin, C. (2023). No equivalence: a new principle of no synonymy. *Constructions*, 15, 1–16.

Leclercq, B., & Morin, C. (2024). Taxonomy of constructional meanings. [Research project on OSF]. doi.org/10.17605/OSF.IO/USRWY.

Leclercq, B., & Morin, C. (2025). The TDD construction. [Research project on OSF]. doi.org/10.17605/OSF.IO/WTVA3.

Lee-Goldman, R. R. (2011). *Context in constructions*. Ph.D. thesis, University of California, Berkeley.

Lehar, S. (2002). *The World in Your Head: A Gestalt View of the Mechanism of Conscious Experience*. Mahwah, NJ: Lawrence Erlbaum Associates.

Leino, J. (2013). Information structure. In T. Hoffmann & G. Trousdale, eds., *The Oxford Handbook of Construction Grammar*. Oxford: Oxford University Press, pp. 329–344.

Leino, J. & Östman, J.-O. (2005). Constructions and variability. In M. Fried & H. Boas, eds., *Grammatical Constructions: Back to the Roots*. Amsterdam: John Benjamins, pp. 191–213.

Lemmens, M. (2016). Cognitive semantics. In N. Riemer, ed., *The Routledge Handbook of Semantics*. Abingdon: Routledge, pp. 90–105.

Lemmens, M. (2017). A cognitive, usage-based view on lexical pragmatics: Response to Hall. In I. Depraetere & R. Salkie, eds., *Semantics and*

Pragmatics: Drawing a Line. Berlin: Springer International Publishing, pp. 101–114.

Levinson, S. C. (1992). Activity types and language. In P. Drew & J. Heritage, eds., *Talk at Work*. Cambridge: Cambridge University Press, 66100, [1979].

Levshina, N. (2022). *Communicative Efficiency: Language Structure and Use*. Cambridge: Cambridge University Press.

Levshina, N. & Lorenz, D. (2022). Communicative efficiency and the principle of no synonymy: Predictability effects and the variation of want to and wanna. *Language and Cognition*, 14(2), 249–274.

Littlemore, J. (2015). *Metonymy: Hidden Shortcuts in Thought, Language, and Communication*. Cambridge: Cambridge University Press.

Littlemore J. (2022). On the creative use of metonymy. *Review of Cognitive Linguistics*, 20(1), 104–129.

Lorenz, D. (2013). *Contractions of English semi-modals: the emancipating effect of frequency*. PhD thesis, Albert-Ludwigs-Universität Freiburg, Freiburg.

Lyngfelt, B., Borin, L., Ohara, K. & Torrent, T., eds. (2018). *Constructicography: Constructicon Development across Languages*. Amsterdam: John Benjamins.

MacWhinney, B. (1989). Competition and lexical categorization. In R. Corrigan, F. Eckman & M. Noonan, eds., *Linguistic Categorization*, Amsterdam: John Benjamins, pp. 195–242.

Marchand, H. (1969). *The Categories and Types of Present-Day English Word Formation. A Synchronic-Diachronic Approach*. Muenchen: Beck'sche Verlagsbuchhandlung.

Mervis, C. & Rosch, E. (1981). Categorization of natural objects. *Annual Review of Psychology*, 32, 89–115.

Michaelis, L. A. (2004). Type shifting in construction grammar: An integrated approach to aspectual coercion. *Cognitive Linguistics*, 15, 1–67.

Mikkelsen, O. & Morin, C. (in press). Register as a source of non-equivalent constructions: be going to and gonna in British English. *English Language and Linguistics*, 29(3).

Moore, R. L. (2004). We're *cool*, mom and dad are *swell*: Basic slang and generational shifts in values. *American Speech*, 79(1), 59–86.

Morin, C. (in press). Are phonemes constructions? A plea for distinguishing function and meaning. *Constructions and Frames*.

Morin, C. (2023). *Social meaning in construction grammar: Double modals in dialects of English*. PhD thesis, Université Paris-Cité, Paris.

Morin, C. & Leclercq, B. (in press). Cognitive Construction Grammar. In Wen, X. & Sinha, C., eds., *The Cambridge Encyclopedia of Cognitive Linguistics*, Cambridge: Cambridge University Press.

Morin, C., Desagulier, G. & Grieve, J. (2024). A social turn for construction grammar: double modals on British Twitter. *English Language and Linguistics*, 8(2), 275–303.

Narrog, H. (2012). Beyond intersubjectification: Textual usages of modality and mood in subordinate clauses as part of speech orientation. *English Text Construction*, 5(1), 29–52.

Narrog, H. (2015). (Inter)subjectification and its limits in secondary grammaticalization. *Language Sciences*, 47, 148–160.

Narrog, H. (2017). Three types of subjectivity, three types of intersubjectivity, their dynamicization and a synthesis. In D. Van Olmen, H. Cuyckens & L. Ghesquière, eds., *Aspects of Grammaticalization: (Inter)Subjectification and Directionality*. Berlin: Mouton de Gruyter, pp. 19–46.

Nathan, G. (2006). Is the phoneme usage-based? Some issues. *International Journal of English Studies*, 6(2), 173–194.

Nesset, T. (2008). *Abstract Phonology in a Concrete Model: Cognitive Linguistics and the Morphology-Phonology Interface*. Berlin: Mouton de Gruyter.

Nikiforidou, K. (2009). Constructional analysis. In F. Brisard, J.-O. Östman & J. Verschueren, eds., *Grammar, Meaning and Pragmatics*. Amsterdam: John Benjamins, pp. 16–32.

Noël, D. (2007). Diachronic construction grammar and grammaticalization theory. *Functions of Language*, 14(2), 177–202.

Norde, M. (2009). *Degrammaticalization*. Oxford: Oxford University Press.

Norde, M. (2012). Lehmann's parameters revisited. In K. Davidse, T. Breban, L. Brems & T. Mortelmans, eds., *Grammaticalization and Language Change: New Reflections*. Amsterdam: John Benjamins, pp. 73–110.

Nuyts, J. (2005). Modality: Overview and linguistic issues. In W. Frawley, ed., *The Expression of Modality*. Berlin: Mouton de Gruyter, pp. 1–26.

Partee, B. H. (1995). Lexical semantics and compositionality. In L. Gleitman & M. Liberman, eds., *Language: An Invitation to Cognitive Science*. Cambridge, MA: The MIT Press, pp. 311–360.

Perek, F. (2012). Alternation-based generalizations are stored in the mental grammar: Evidence from a sorting task experiment. *Cognitive Linguistics*, 23, 601–635.

Perek, F. (2016). Using distributional semantics to study syntactic productivity in diachrony: A case study. *Linguistics*, 54(1), 149–188.

Perek, F. (2023). Construction grammar and usage-based theory. In M. Diaz-Campos & S. Balasch, eds., *The Handbook of Usage-Based Linguistics*. Hoboken, NJ: Wiley-Blackwell, pp. 215–231.

Pijpops, D. (2020). What is an alternation? Six answers. *Belgian Journal of Linguistics*, 34, 283–294.

Pisciotta, F. (2024). When constructional choice is a matter of context: *Sembrare*-constructions across a continuum of text genres. *CogniTextes*, 25.

Plank, F. (1984). The modals story retold. *Studies in Language*, 8, 305–366.

Polinsky, M. (1998). A non-syntactic account of some asymmetries in the double object construction. In J.-P. Koenig, ed., *Conceptual Structure and Language: Bridging the Gap*, Stanford, CA: CSLI, pp. 402–423.

Rambelli, G. (2025). *Constructions and Compositionality: Cognitive and Computational Explorations*. Cambridge: Cambridge University Press.

Ratcliff, R., Gomez, P. & McKoon, G. (2004). A diffusion model account of the lexical decision task. *Psychological Review*, 111(1), 159.

Recanati, F. (2004). Pragmatics and semantics. In L. R. Horn & G. Ward, eds., *The Handbook of Pragmatics*. Oxford: Blackwell, pp. 442–462.

Reddy, M. (1979). The conduit metaphor: A case of conflict in our language about language. In A. Ortony, ed., *Metaphor and Thought*. Cambridge: Cambridge University Press, pp. 284–324.

Rhodes, R. (1994). Aural images. In L. Hinton, J. Nichols & J. Ohala, eds., *Sound Symbolism*. Cambridge: Cambridge University Press, pp. 276–92.

Riemer, N. (2010). *Introducing Semantics*. Cambridge: Cambridge University Press.

Sampson, G. (2016). Two ideas of creativity. In M. Hinton, ed., *Evidence, Experiment, and Argument in Linguistics and Philosophy of Language*. Bern: Peter Lang, pp. 15–26.

Schmid, H.-J. (2012). Entrenchment, salience, and basic levels. In D. Geeraerts & H. Cuyckens, eds., *The Oxford Handbook of Cognitive Linguistics*. Oxford: Oxford University Press, pp. 117–138.

Schmid, H.-J. (2014). Lexico-grammatical patterns, pragmatic associations and discourse frequency. In T. Herbst, H.-J. Schmid & S. Faulhaber, eds., *Constructions, Collocations, Patterns*. Berlin: Mouton de Gruyter, pp. 239–293.

Schmid, H.-J. (2020). *The Dynamics of the Linguistic System: Usage, Conventionalization, and Entrenchment*. Oxford: Oxford University Press.

Siewirska, A. & Hollmann, W. (2007). Ditransitive clauses with special reference to Lancashire dialect. In M. Hannay & G. Steen, eds., *Structural-Functional Studies in English Grammar: In Honour of Lachlan Mackenzie*. Amsterdam: John Benjamins, pp. 83–102.

Silvennoinen, O. (2023). Is construction grammar cognitive? *Constructions*, 15, 1–17.

Smirnova, E. (2015). When secondary grammaticalization starts: A look from the constructional perspective. *Language Sciences*, 47(2), 215–228.

Smith, C. (2014). The phonaesthetics of blends: A lexicographic study of cognitive blends in the OED. *ExELL – Explorations in English Language and Linguistics*, 2(1), 12–45.

Sommerer, L. (2020). Why we avoid the 'multiple inheritance' issue in usage-based cognitive construction grammar. *Belgian Journal of Linguistics*, 34, 320–331.

Tagliamonte, S. A., & Pabst, K. (2020). A cool comparison: Adjectives of positive evaluation in Toronto, Canada and York, England. *Journal of English Linguistics*, 48(1), 3–30.

Talmy, L. (1988). Force dynamics in language and cognition. *Cognitive Science*, 12(1), 49–100.

Talmy, L. (2000). *Toward a Cognitive Semantics: Concept Structuring Systems*. Cambridge, MA: The MIT Press.

Thompson, S. A. & Koide, Y. (1987). Iconicity and 'indirect objects' in English. *Journal of Pragmatics*, 11(3), 399–406.

Traugott, E. C. (1995). Subjectification in grammaticalisation. In S. Wright & D. Stein, eds., *Subjectivity and Subjectivisation*. Cambridge: Cambridge University Press, pp. 31–54.

Traugott, E. C. (2002). From etymology to historical pragmatics. In D. Minkova & R. Stockwell, eds., *Studying the History of the English Language: Millennial Perspectives*. Berlin: Mouton de Gruyter, pp. 19–49.

Traugott, E. C. (2003). From subjectification to intersubjectification. In R. Hickey, ed., *Motives for Language Change*. Cambridge: Cambridge University Press, pp. 124–139.

Traugott, E. C. (2008). The grammaticalization of NP of NP patterns. In A. Bergs & G. Diewald, eds., *Constructions and Language Change*. Berlin: Mouton de Gruyter, pp. 21–43.

Traugott, E. C. (2010). (Inter)subjectivity and (inter)subjectification: A reassessment. In K. Davidse, L. Vandelanotte & H. Cuyckens, eds., *Subjectification, Intersubjectification and Grammaticalization*. Berlin: Mouton de Gruyter, pp. 29–71.

Traugott, E. C. (2015). Toward a coherent account of grammatical constructionalization. In J. Barðdal, E. Smirnova, L. Sommerer & S. Gildea, eds., *Diachronic Construction Grammar*. Amsterdam: John Benjamins, pp. 51–79.

Traugott, E. C. (2024). Rethinking the relationship between subjectification, intersubjectification, and textualization from a constructionalist perspective. *Cognitive Semantics*, 10(1), 1–32.

Traugott, E. C., & Trousdale, G. (2013). *Constructionalization and Constructional Changes*. Oxford: Oxford University Press.

Trips, C. (2009). *Lexical Semantics and Diachronic Morphology: The Development of -hood, -dom and -ship in the History of English*. Tübingen: Max Niemeyer Verlag.

Trousdale, G. (2008a). Constructions in grammaticalization and lexicalization: Evidence from a composite predicate in the history of English. In G. Trousdale & N. Gisborne, eds., *Constructional Approaches to English Grammar*. Berlin: Mouton de Gruyter, pp. 33–67.

Trousdale, G. (2008b). Words and constructions in grammaticalization: The end of the English impersonal construction. In S. M. Fitzmaurice & D. Minkova, eds., *Studies in the History of the English Language IV: Empirical and Analytical Advances in the Study of English Language Change*. Berlin: Mouton de Gruyter, pp. 301–326.

Trousdale, G. (2010). Issues in constructional approaches to grammaticalization. In K. Stathi, E. Gehweiler & E. König, eds., *Grammaticalization: Current Views and Issues*. Amsterdam: John Benjamins, pp. 51–71.

Trousdale, G. (2012). Grammaticalization, constructions, and the grammaticalization of constructions. In K. Davidse, T. Breban, L. Brems & T. Mortelmans, eds., *Grammaticalization and Language Change: New Reflections*. Amsterdam: Benjamins, pp. 167–198.

Turner, M. (1991). *Reading Minds: The Study of English in the Age of Cognitive Science*. Princeton, NJ: Princeton University Press.

Uhrig, P. (2015). Why the principle of no synonymy is overrated. *Zeitschrift für Anglistik und Amerikanistic*, 63(3), 323–37.

Uhrig, P. (2020). Creative intentions: The fine line between "creative" and "wrong." *Cognitive Semiotics*, 13(1), 1–19.

Ungerer, T. (2023). A gradient notion of constructionhood. *Constructions*, 15(1), 1–20.

Ungerer, T. & Hartmann, S. (2023). *Constructionist Approaches: Past, Present, Future*. Cambridge: Cambridge University Press.

Välimaa-Blum, R. (2005) *Cognitive Phonology in Construction Grammar: Analytic Tools for Students of English*. Berlin: Mouton de Gruyter.

Weber, T. & Kopf, K. (2023). Free variation, unexplained variation? In K. Kopf & T. Weber, eds., *Free Variation in Grammar: Empirical and Theoretical Approaches*, Amsterdam: John Benjamins, pp. 1–20.

Wen, X. (2022). Construction pragmatics: A brief sketch. In *Lege Artis. Language Yesterday, Today, Tomorrow*, 7(1), 249–266.

Willich, A. (2022). Introducing construction semantics (CxS): a frame-semantic extension of construction grammar and constructicography. *Linguistics Vanguard*, 8(1). 139–149.

Wilson, D. & Sperber, D. (2002). Truthfulness and relevance. *Mind*, 111, 583–632.

Winter, B. & Perek, F. (2023). Cognitive linguistics. In L. Wei, Z. Hua & J. Simpson, eds., *The Routledge Handbook of Applied Linguistics*. Abingdon: Routledge, pp. 309–321.

Yoon, S. (2012). *Constructions, semantic compatibility, and coercion: An empirical usage-based approach*. Ph.D. thesis, Rice University, Houston.

Zadeh, L. (1965). Fuzzy sets. *Information and Control*, 8, 338–353.

Zipf, G. K. (1949). *Human Behavior and the Principle of Least Effort*. Cambridge, MA: Addison-Wesley Press.

Construction Grammar

Thomas Hoffmann
Catholic University of Eichstätt-Ingolstadt

Thomas Hoffmann is Full Professor and Chair of English Language and Linguistics at the Catholic University of Eichstätt-Ingolstadt. His main research interests are usage-based Construction Grammar, language variation and change and linguistic creativity. He has published widely in international journals such as *Cognitive Linguistics, English Language and Linguistics,* and *English World-Wide*. His monographs *Preposition Placement in English* (2011) and *English Comparative Correlatives: Diachronic and Synchronic Variation at the Lexicon-Syntax Interface* (2019) were both published by Cambridge University Press. His textbook on *Construction Grammar: The Structure of English* (2022) as well as an Element on *The Cognitive Foundation of Post-colonial Englishes: Construction Grammar as the Cognitive Theory for the Dynamic Model* (2021) have also both been published with Cambridge University Press. He is also co-editor (with Graeme Trousdale) of *The Oxford Handbook of Construction Grammar* (2013, Oxford University Press).

Alexander Bergs
Osnabrück University

Alexander Bergs joined the Institute for English and American Studies at Osnabrück University, Germany, in 2006 when he became Full Professor and Chair of English Language and Linguistics. His research interests include, among others, language variation and change, constructional approaches to language, the role of context in language, the syntax/pragmatics interface, and cognitive poetics. His works include several authored and edited books (*Social Networks and Historical Sociolinguistics, Modern Scots, Contexts and Constructions, Constructions and Language Change*), a short textbook on *Synchronic English Linguistics*, one on *Understanding Language Change* (with Kate Burridge) and the two-volume *Handbook of English Historical Linguistics* (ed. with Laurel Brinton; now available as five-volume paperback) as well as more than fifty papers in high-profile international journals and edited volumes. Alexander Bergs has taught at the Universities of Düsseldorf, Bonn, Santiago de Compostela, Wisconsin-Milwaukee, Catania, Vigo, Thessaloniki, Athens, and Dalian and has organized numerous international workshops and conferences.

About the Series

Construction Grammar is the leading cognitive theory of syntax. The present Elements series will survey its theoretical building blocks, show how Construction Grammar can capture various linguistic phenomena across a wide range of typologically different languages, and identify emerging frontier topics from a theoretical, empirical and applied perspective.

For EU product safety concerns, contact us at Calle de José Abascal, 56–1°,
28003 Madrid, Spain or eugpsr@cambridge.org.